CONTEMPORARY
BATIK AND TIE-DYE

CONTEMPORARY
BATIK AND
TIE-DYE

Methods · Inspiration · Dyes

BY DONA Z. MEILACH

CROWN PUBLISHERS, INC., NEW YORK

Printed in the United States of America
Published simultaneously in Canada by
General Publishing Company Limited

Seventh Printing, October, 1975

Designed by Shari de Miskey

ACKNOWLEDGMENTS

I wish to extend my deep and sincere gratitude to everyone who helped in compiling information for this book. My sincere thanks to the more than four hundred artists who responded with photos, long letters, and information about their processes. Special thanks, too, to those who shipped their work to me for photography. I wish I could have used all of the sixteen hundred photos that I took and more than five hundred that were submitted.

The attitude of generously sharing experiences in this expanding art form was evident and gratifying. I especially want to thank the following who demonstrated their techniques while I photographed them at work and tape-recorded their comments: Mr. Bill Hinz of the Art Institute of Chicago for the series in the chapter on Direct Application of Dyes; Mr. Stephen Blumrich for his painstaking work with multiple dippings, and Miss Ellen Fisher for several of the tie-dye demonstrations.

I am especially delighted to have made a lifelong friendship through the arts with Mrs. Joyce Wexler, Beverly Hills, California, who demonstrated the batik with paper collage series. In addition, an informal batik symposium held at Mrs. Wexler's home with teachers and artists from the Los Angeles area resulted in a cross-fertilization of ideas that was invaluable to everyone.

I appreciate the cooperation of Mrs. Lucille Bealmer, Textile Department, Northern Illinois University, DeKalb, Illinois; Mrs. Blanche Carstenson, Avila College, Kansas City, Missouri; Sister Mary Remy Revor, Mount Mary College, Milwaukee, Wisconsin; and Miss Esther Robinson, Oak Park High School, Oak Park, Illinois, who permitted me to photograph students at work.

Chemical advice and assistance in translating technical symbols and formulas into layman's language was freely given by Mr. Ed Elder, American Aniline Products, Chicago, Illinois; Mr. Joseph DiLorenzo and Mr. Snehal Desae, Keystone Aniline and Chemical Company, Chicago, Illinois, and Mr. John Ferrara, Palos Heights, Illinois.

Mr. Joseph Evilsizer and Mr. Michael Flynn of Fibrec, San Francisco, California, and Mr. Gerry Frericks of Putnam Dyes, Quincy, Illinois, were general fonts of invaluable sources and information and I am happy to have them as friends.

A sincere thank you to Mr. and Mrs. Jim Burton and Jan Wagstaff, of Durable Arts, San Rafael, California, for their friendship, help, and information about pigments and new products applicable to batik. Thanks, too, to the staff of Binney & Smith, makers of Crayola, and to Mr. Dan Price of CPC International for creating specific projects adaptable to this book.

My excellence award goes to Mr. Ben Lavitt, Astra Photo, Chicago, Illinois, for his unflagging insistence on perfection in the photography and for processing all photos to achieve the best possible reproductions. And a typing award goes to Marilyn Regula who creates perfectly typed pages from my marked up sheets of paper.

Eternal gratitude is due my editor, Mr. Brandt Aymar, and my husband, Dr. Melvin Meilach, who offered continued support and encouragement during the long gestation period of this book.

Note: All photographs by Dona and Mel Meilach unless otherwise credited.

FOREWORD

To the beginner, batik and tie-dye processes may seem mysterious and magical. In a way they are. We should hope, to some extent, they always will remain that way. That's the continuing challenge, the charm, and attraction of dyeing materials by these resist techniques. Watching colored water roll off the waxed surface of a batik fabric and observing the unwaxed area of the material change colors is constantly fascinating, and different fabrics make every batik a new experience.

In tie-dye, when you undo the wrapped, gathered, and knotted fabrics, there is a sense of discovery. You anxiously wonder if all the ties took as planned, and then you observe the creeping color that cannot be planned and is always so beautiful.

The book is arranged so you can refer to the batik directions in chapters 2 and 3 and progress into color mixing, design principles, and other approaches to batik. Basic tie-dye methods are illustrated in chapter 11 using ties for overall patterns, circles, folds, sewing, clamping, and more. Ideas for combining the designs are abundant along with scores of ideas for using the fabrics with other media and in a multitude of ways.

Once you are familiar with batik and tie-dye procedures, your most important considerations will be which dyes to use and how to overdye colors.

Dyes and How to Use Them, chapter 14, applies to both batik and tie-dye. Become familiar with the chapter and refer to it often. It is impossible to absorb all there is to know about the various dyes in one reading. The information about dye classes, which to use for what fabrics, and the dye chart, will remove the mystery that has shrouded dye chemistry for too many years.

To avoid the frustration of muddy colors for your projects, important advice is to *always measure the amount of dye powder you use.* You will save time, effort, and dye. All measures are offered in teaspoons, tablespoons, and kitchen equivalents so they are easy to calculate for any amount of fabric. Most people tend to use a package of dye for every project no matter what size the material. For small, thin pieces of fabric such as a square yard of silk, you need only about one-half teaspoon of each color so a package of dye can be used for many projects. For color overdyeing, refer to the chart and the color wheel in chapter 4.

Don't expect perfection. Don't feel that your one-of-a-kind, hand-designed, hand-dyed pieces have to simulate store-bought fabrics. They won't and they shouldn't. That's what makes them unique and individually yours. Above all, enjoy doing batik and tie-dye. The processes are fun and exciting. The potential for using them is unlimited.

Dona Z. Meilach
Palos Heights, Illinois

CONTENTS

CONTEMPORARY
BATIK AND TIE-DYE

SUN. Enza Quargnali. 116 inches high, 54 inches wide. White, green, and black on cotton. The crackle, or heavy veining, throughout is a characteristic of batik.
Photo, Philip Sibley

1

INTRODUCTION—
THE RESIST PROCESSES

TODAY's artists, constantly developing innovative areas for expression, are stimulating new approaches to textile arts. Batik and tie-dye, as new as they are ancient, are capturing tremendous attention. They are being explored, updated, and combined in highly imaginative ways. The impetus is aided by advances in modern dye technology that offer easy-to-use dyestuffs in brilliant colors that are relatively permanent and colorfast on a variety of natural fibers.

Batik and tie-dye are considered "resist" techniques. This means that some portions of the fabric are prepared to "resist" color when dye is applied. In batik, the resist material traditionally used is molten wax. In tie-dye, the ties, folds, and knots resist the colorants.

The word "batik" is Indonesian and means "wax writing." Briefly, the process involves brushing on melted paraffin and beeswax so it penetrates specific portions of the fabric. The waxed fabric is then dipped into or painted with wet dyes. The waxed areas repel or "resist" the dyes; thus the term "resist" process. Each time a new dye color is introduced on the fabric, portions of that color are waxed and held until the desired color scheme is achieved. All wax is removed by ironing the fabric between papers; the heat of the iron melts the wax which is absorbed by the papers. Modern adaptations of this basic technique, the fabrics, resists, and dyes used are fully explored in the chapters on batik and dyes.

You may often recognize batik by its characteristic crackle, or veining, that appears throughout the design and unifies the colors and composition. It results when the cooled wax is cracked to allow the dye to penetrate. Some artists prefer to minimize and even eliminate the characteristic crackle and this requires special care and extra waxings. Recently available resin resists and waxes that are very flexible can be used to reduce crackle.

Tie-dye is accomplished by knotting, binding, folding, and/or sewing the fabric. Portions of the material that are tightly tied with string, rubber bands, plastic, wire, and other materials reject, or resist, the color when the material

The batik process consists of brushing melted wax on fabric that will subsequently be immersed in dye. The waxed areas will resist the color.

Tie-dye consists of tying up fabric, then immersing it in dyes. The areas that are tightly tied resist the color: these result in the circles illustrated at right.

is immersed in the dyebath. Variations of tie-dyeing methods are numerous. Objects such as rice, seeds, corks, washers, beads, stones, and tin cans may be tied into the fabric. Portions of folded fabrics may be clamped between shaped pieces of wood for designs that repeat the wood shapes. Folded and tied areas can be squirted with dyes. Parts of the fabric may be wrapped in plastic to resist dye.

Tie-dye fabrics exhibit unusual textures caused by the dyes as they creep around the ties that protect parts of the cloth. The assortment of patterns that can be created by variations and combinations of the ties, folds, and wraps is endless. Fabrics can be tied and dyed one color, untied, then retied a slightly different way and redyed another color. The steps can be repeated several times for infinite arrangements, patterns, color values, and textures.

LADIES WITH MIRRORS.   Ethyl Wirtshafter. 25 inches high, 30 inches wide. White, yellow, pink, and navy blue on linen. Batiks often have a painterly quality and the crackle can be seen throughout the design.

RADIANCE *(detail)*.   Bernice Colman. Tie-dyed circles have a spidery linear feeling achieved by tying the fabric with cords that are not wound too closely together, allowing the dyes to creep into the fabric under some of the ties.

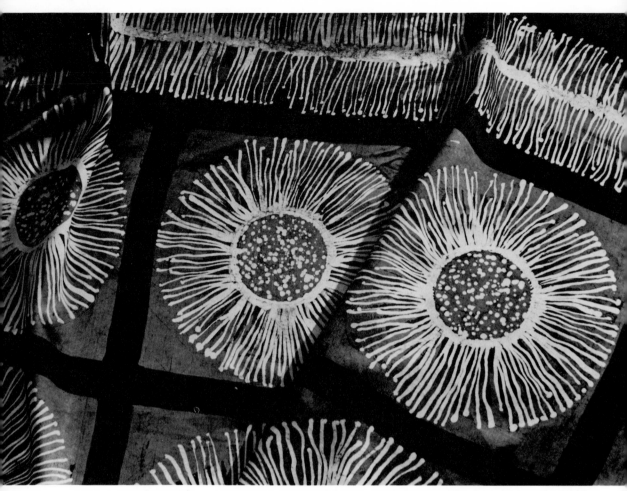

SUNFLOWER. Sister Mary Remy Revor. A batik with very little crackle is created by applying dyes directly to the fabric rather than dipping waxed fabric into dye. Very controlled lines and shapes can be achieved by applying the wax with a tjanting tool (page 56) originally used by the Javanese.

Photo, John Ahlhauser

Tie-dyeing gained popularity in the United States in the past decade among young people who quickly adapted the easy-to-do method for individualizing their shirts, jeans, and casual clothing. Now, artists are recognizing that the circles, pleats, gathers, and knots have a much broader potential. The examples in the tie-dye chapters attest to the imaginative use of the fabrics in a stunning array of wall hangings, sculpture, interior decorations, and high fashion clothing.

An additional practice associated with the two techniques is referred to as "discharge" dyeing. This means that you begin the resist process on a dark fabric. The waxed or tied fabric is then immersed in a bleach solution or color remover (instead of a dye) and color is discharged; hence the term, "discharge" dyeing. Interesting effects can result by coloring a fabric with dyes, then dipping portions of the colored areas in a bleach solution to remove some of

Tie-dye *(detail).* Circles and stripes can be arranged asymmetrically. For texture and dimension, the resulting puckers are often allowed to remain without ironing the fabric.

DIAMONDS *(detail).* Charlotte White. Fold-dye on silk results in a symmetrical, geometric pattern.

Courtesy, artist

the color and yield subtle shades. Sometimes the bleaches will separate blended colors and nuances result that cannot always be predicted or accomplished in other ways.

Artists already exploring batik and tie-dye have discovered that both the similarities and differences of the two methods can be exploited so that combining them promises new dimensions for textile decoration. They may be used with block printing, silk screening, and direct application of dyes and paints.

Perhaps the most important ingredient of these art forms, other than design, rests with the dyes that are available and how they are used. Working with dyes and their formulas is similar to experimenting with new cooking recipes. There is no substitute for buying and mixing the components yourself, and testing the results on different fabrics to learn what appeals to you most. All dye information is in chapter 14 at the back of the book for easy reference.

Resist dye on linen *(fragment)*. Egyptian / Byzantine Period, first half sixth century. The figures and their placement in rows and between columns is an application, in textiles, of the designs on ivory carvings of the period.
Courtesy, The Cleveland Museum of Art,
Purchase from the John H. Wade Fund

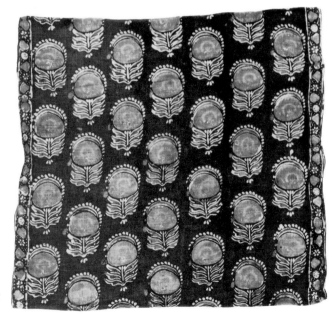

SCARF. India, nineteenth century *(detail)*. Cotton resist print.
Courtesy, Los Angeles County Museum of Art

An Indonesian batik tjap; an instrument made of copper strips adhered to a frame and used for applying repeat wax patterns to a fabric. The tjap is dipped in wax and then the wax stamped onto the fabric thus creating the resist design.
Collection: Ronald Jué

HISTORY OF BATIK

The ancient history of textiles tends to be sketchy because fabrics disintegrate in time and from weather. The exact origins of batik are uncertain. Fragments, probably of Indian origin, have been found in first century Egyptian tombs. One theory is that the batik method was indigenous to the Indian archipelago and spread from there to the Western world. Another theory is supported by evidence that it existed—and may have originated— in Asia and then spread to the Malaysian area. Examples of eighth century batik screens, probably by Chinese artists, are preserved in Japan's Nara Museum.

Whatever its origin, batik was a highly accomplished art form in Java and Bali by the thirteenth century as a pastime for fine ladies. The hand-decorated fabrics first appeared in costumes of the aristocracy and were soon used in clothing worn by the entire court. As more fabrics were demanded for clothes, servants were called upon to help in the preparation of the fabric, in dyeing and, eventually, for design waxing.

Specific, readily recognizable motifs, patterns, and colors developed. Often one design identified one family or an area. As exports and trade routes opened, Javanese batiks were introduced first to Holland and then to other parts of Europe about the seventeenth century. In England, when the process was introduced, industrialists were already printing fabrics reasonably. They attempted to produce imitation batiks on a large scale but the cost was prohibitive. At first they used vegetable dyes; then after the 1860s, when synthetic dyes were available, the process became more feasible. The major difficulty—to print the haphazard crackle mechanically—was eventually overcome, but not too efficiently or convincingly. Some of the batiks were strongly influenced by the Art Nouveau styles that spread throughout Europe in the early 1900s and we know them from the collections of the greats of that period, A. H. Mackmurdo, C. R. Mackintosh, and Roger Fry.

In Germany, during the early 1900s, elaborate evening gowns of batik

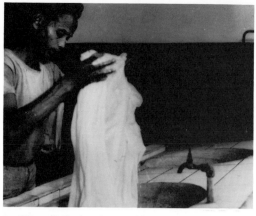

1. The cloth is thoroughly washed in clean water to remove any starch and sizing. It is then carefully restarched just enough to control the application of wax. Javanese batiks are waxed front and back rather than through the materials as is the practice in the United States. The fabric is smoothed by beating with a wooden hammer.

2. The design is drawn and the first waxing is accomplished with the patterned tjap; lines and additional details may be waxed in with the tjanting. This waxing will resist color; all waxed areas will remain white.

3. After the fabric has been dyed, the wax is removed by scraping.

4. The second pattern of waxing is applied using another patterned tjap.

6. Following all dye processes the fabric is dipped in boiling water to remove wax. It is pressed and ready for use.

All photos, courtesy Batik Research Institute, Jogjakarta, Indonesia

5. The wax is again removed after the second dyeing.

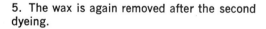

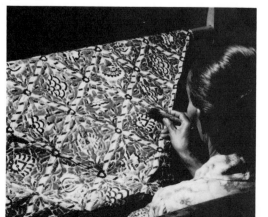

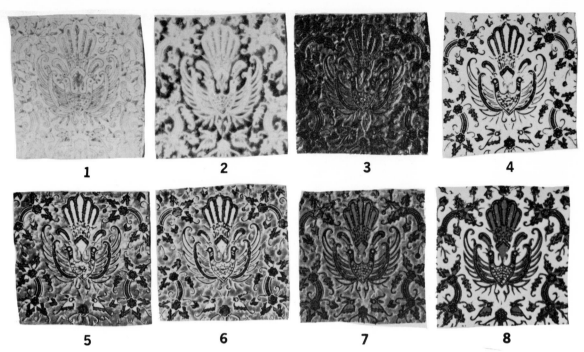

In Indonesia, batik proceeds along the traditional methods at left. Actual swatches of the material show the changes at each step which has a name in Javanese.

1. The design is drawn (Nglowong) with wax using a tjanting and sometimes a tjap. It is waxed on both sides of the fabric.
2. The design is thickly covered with wax on both sides (Nembok). All areas not to be dyed are waxed.
3. The first dyeing is in a blue dye (Medel).
4. The first coatings of wax are removed from parts that are to be dyed with the brown color (Ngerok). A dull knife is used to scrape the wax which has been purposely formulated so it will not be too sticky, yet it will resist the dye.
5. Additional wax is applied to the design where the blue is to be retained (Mbironi).
6. The fabric is waxed in all brown and blue areas. It is difficult to detect in photos, but the wax is thickly encrusted on the fabric in tiny dots and shapes.
7. The fabric is dyed brown (Njoga) by soaking it in a "soga" dyestuff solution.
8. Wax has been removed (Nglorod) by soaking in boiling water; it is ironed, ready for use, and called a "kain batik."

Fabrics: courtesy First Editions,
San Jose, Calif.

fabrics were highly fashionable. Popular, too, were curtains that gave a stained-glass effect because some of the wax was purposely left in the fabric. The Germans developed glass and metal tjantings and an electrically heated wax writing pencil that could adjust the flow of wax for thick and thin lines. The craft moved over Europe and again imitation batiks were in vogue, created, produced, and exported by industry. The imitations were clever. The machine-printed fabrics even emulated the bleeding edges of the dye designs that were characteristic of home-dyed fabrics. But by the 1920s economic difficulties beset the textile industry in Europe and commercial batiks were no longer produced.

Following World War II and the establishment of a Republic of Indonesia, the Javanese batik industry was revitalized. Cooperatives were established for

◄

Photos at left illustrate several of the steps involved in the traditional Javanese preparation of batik. The samples above illustrate the changes in the material at various steps.

UNTITLED. Gloria Perrino. Red and white tie-dye developed with batik in navy blue. 41 inches high, 36 inches wide. Batik, studied in Java, is given a modern interpretation by an American artist.

Courtesy, artist

the production of batiks under communal control. Government help and direction were given and today a Batik Research Institute exists at Jogjakarta, Indonesia.

The majority of Javanese batiks today still are produced by traditional methods in blue and soga brown (a distinctive color rarely found outside Java). Motifs are a carryover from the earlier centuries and include symbolic designs of birds, butterflies, heraldic devices, floral patterns in overall prints. Established patterns have names, such as "parang" which means "rugged rock" and usually has diagonal craggy lines or stripes. A "kawang" pattern is made of ovals that represent the fruit and leaf of the kapok tree and the motifs are arranged in groups of four. They are laboriously made by the processes described on page 11. The wax coating is boiled off after each dyebath and then the entire piece is rewaxed. Sometimes one length of fabric requires months to complete. It is these designs that are usually associated with Javanese batiks.

Recently, a few artists abandoned traditional attitudes and adopted contemporary painterly concepts with hints of the exotic shapes often associated

THE FACES *(detail)*. Kuwat and Soemihardjo. Contemporary Javanese batiks resemble painting styles, using tiny dots and circles in a modern interpretation of Javanese design. To apply wax, tjantings, spoons, spatulas, syringes, and brushes are used. The color scheme is often limited to only two or three colors.

Courtesy, First Editions, San Jose, Calif.

with Indian temples, Javanese dance, and folklore. The fabrics are not necessarily for practical use, but are often framed as paintings and mounted as wall hangings. They are unquestionably modern, with a distinct and lilting Oriental flavor.

As this change in Javanese batik is occurring, American and European artists, traveling to and living in Java, are learning the processes and bringing them back. In the United States batik courses are being added to school textile art curricula. The designs and uses for the fabrics are bound to cause a new chapter to be written in the history of batik.

The trend is to decorate the fabric any way the artist envisions; to apply design by any method, traditional or innovative, and even depart from standard procedures. The fabrics are for clothing, hangings, furnishings, relief, and stuffed sculpture. An important observation is that batik no longer is considered a "pure" art but one which can be combined with other media and methods. The driving force for the artist is to apply the technique for the end desired, rather than allowing the technique to control the artist as an end in itself.

COAT. Rita L. Shumaker. Clothing is a popular, practical application for batik fabrics, providing colorfast dyes are used. Four-color coat of white organdy in yellow, fuchsia, orange, and wine.

Photo, John Daughtry

DRESS *(back)*. John Mulder. Batik on silk. Fabric pieces were cut, then batiked before sewing together. Dress design, Phyllis Mulder.

REJOICE.   Candace Johnson. Batik wall hanging. 6 feet high, 5 feet wide.
Courtesy, artist

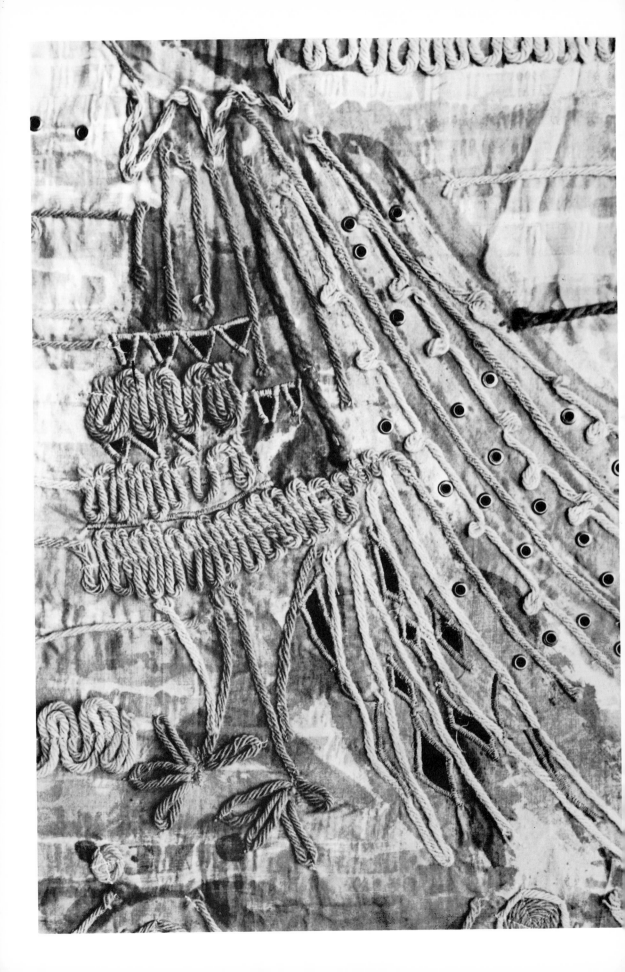

MERCEDES-BENZ MOTOR.   Kathleen Knipple. Stuffed batik wall relief actual size of automobile motor. Inkodye on Indian Head cotton.

Courtesy, artist

◄

ROOSTERS *(detail)*.   Karen Chang. A brightly colored batik fabric is further decorated with yarn, eyelets, and cutout areas that have been machine-buttonhole-bound.

HISTORY OF TIE-DYE

The practice of tie-dyeing fabrics has been used in almost all parts of the world at some time. Tie-dyed fabric remnants reveal a history that probably began in ancient Asia and spread down the sub-Indian continent to Malaya and across Africa. Relics of such textiles also date from burial grounds in China and Persia along the ancient caravan and silk routes.

There is evidence that tie-dye was used in the early Chinese T'ang Dynasty (A.D. 618–906). From there it spread to Japan where the beautiful silk fabrics, so highly prized, were tie-dyed for clothing of the nobility and priests. When cottons and cotton fabrics were introduced hundreds of years later (in the nineteenth century), common people were finally able to practice the craft also. Soon after, industrialization took over and the homecraft dye industry was no more.

Tie-dye was probably well developed in India earlier than in Japan. Clothing of the people depicted in fresco paintings in the caves at Ajanta, Hyderabad (A.D. sixth and seventh centuries), have white circular patterns similar to those made by tying circles known in India as "plangi." These circles varied in size. Very tiny circles were made by placing damp fabric on a bed of nails. Girls with extraordinarily long fingernails would pick up the points of the fabric and tie them, often using a continuous thread to create a line from one dot to another.

Examples of tie-dyed fabrics also exist from Thailand and Cambodia; indications are that it spread from there to Indonesia. It is still a prevailing method for decorating fine silks used for shawls, veils, and sarongs for men and women of Java and Bali.

African nations have used tie-dye methods for years and still do. Many Americans practicing the craft today learned natural dye recipes while serving in the Peace Corps among these peoples. They also brought back bolder design concepts than those that originated in the Indonesian and Oriental cultures.

Tie-dyed textiles from each country exhibit distinguishing design and color characteristics by which scholars have been able to chart the origin and types of fabrics produced throughout the world at different times in a particular culture.

The earliest tie-dyes on the American continent date from pre-Columbian times when circles and squares were repeated as simple one color patterns. Other pieces have been credited to Mexico, Guatemala, Peru, Bolivia, Paraguay, and Argentina. In North America the Pueblo and other Indian tribes used the craft at a much later time.

The techniques employed by different peoples throughout the centuries vary and yet have many similarities. The cloth used accounts for some of the variation: fine cloth is more adaptable to fine binding and small patterns; heavier cloth lends itself best to larger patterns.

In every culture the techniques are basically the same. The cloth is tied, knotted, bound, folded, and stitched. Sewing, referred to as "tritik," has tremendous variations. The thread is sewn through one or more layers of fabric and one end is knotted; the thread is then drawn up until the fabric is held tightly together in closely packed pleats or folds. The direction

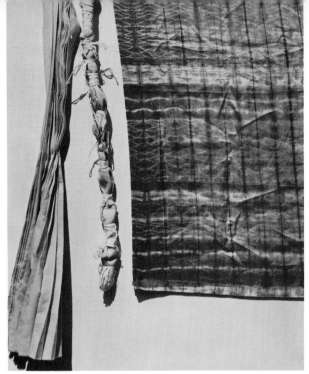

A striped effect with spidery lines is achieved by first accordion folding fabric and then tying it to create the horizontal stripes. The material used for tying and the way it is wound determine the character of the stripe. (Blanche Carstenson)

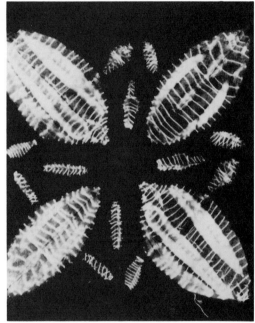

An example of stitching or tritik. The two layers of a folded fabric were stitched over the fold. The threads were pulled tightly and the fabric immersed in dye. When the threads are removed the latticelike pattern results. (Grace Earl)

of the sewing in circles, ovals, lines, and so forth determines the direction of the dyed pattern; and also gives a jagged, staccato effect to the line.

Dyeing only parts of the tied fabric at a time creates panels of color. In some countries pointed wood pegs are used to push up parts of the cloth to ½ inch or more. These projecting pegs are tied with waxed thread to yield large undyed patches of fabric against the dyed background.

One other approach deserves mention because it is becoming increasingly popular. *Ikat* is a Malaysian word describing a technique in which the yarn is tied and dyed before it is woven, as distinct from the whole fabric. Depending upon the yarn used, an ikat weaving may be an allover blend of colors, or, in hard yarns where the color does not creep so much, the pattern can be tightly controlled.

All the techniques developed throughout the centuries are still in use by today's craftsmen along with new approaches and combinations. Evidence indicates that tie-dye does not depend on how many ties one can do, but how they are related within the space of the overall fabric and how effectively the colors interplay.

Panel of embroidered tie-dyed satin (India, nineteenth century).
Courtesy, Los Angeles County Museum of Art

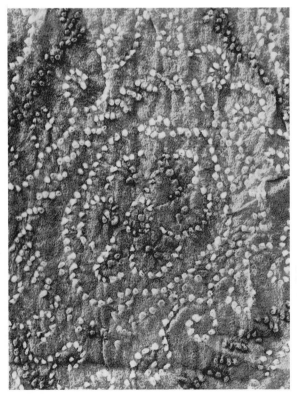

Detail of a silk chiffon scarf (India). The tiny dots of a contemporary tie-dye use an old technique: a pattern of nails is placed beneath the cloth; the fabric is lifted from the points and each circle is individually tied; the pucker remains in the fabric.

A modern tie-dyed cotton pullover shirt from Africa is made with a circular pattern of tiny connecting tie-dyed dots.

Detail illustrates the practice of tying small portions of the fabric with connecting threads that are pulled tightly to result in an overall pattern. You can observe the difference in design from the scarf (opposite) in which each dot is tied but no threads connect the dots.

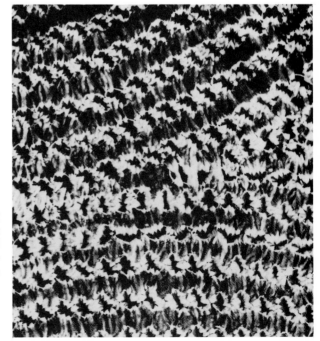

HANGING.   Pat Obye. Circles, stripes, and sewing are combined in this modern approach to tie-dye.

HANGING.   Marian Clayden. Fiber reactive dyes on linen. 70 inches
high, 50 inches wide.

Dress and man's tunic. Rita L. Shumaker. Velveteen tie-dye and fold-dye discharge. Dark brown fabric had color removed to result in a copperlike tortoiseshell shade in the patterned areas.

Photo, John Daughtry
Collection, Mr. & Mrs. Isaac Luski, Charlotte, N.C.

Tie-dyed fabrics with easily recognizable tie patterns are fashioned into high style clothing. Fabrics include sheer silk chiffon, cotton, velveteen, and heavy cotton.

Courtesy, Dylon International Ltd.

PODS. Rita L. Shumaker. Fold-dye on lavender cotton broad-cloth; burgundy and brown over-dyes. 48 inches high, 24 inches wide. Two-sided room divider with hand-dyed yarn worked into macramé knots and beads.

Photo, Floyd Simmons

▶

INDIAN IMAGE. Beth Ford. Batik center panel, tie-dye at top and bottom, on muslin. Yarn is woven to hold pieces together and fur scraps are woven into open areas. 8 feet high, 4 feet wide. Beige, brown, blue gray, and black on white.

Photo, Judy Durick

2

BEGINNING TO BATIK

THE best way to understand how batik works is to do it. Explanations of how to do batik do not prepare you for the almost magical changes that occur when the waxed fabrics are dipped into different color dyebaths. So gather your materials and begin. You can work in your kitchen or laundry area. The materials suggested for your first batik are readily available. The color scheme is limited to two shades of one color and a third color which involves three dippings. Consider your first batik a "sampler," a way of familiarizing yourself with the method. It could turn out to be a masterpiece, too.

The general procedures for batik involve four basic steps. Each is discussed and illustrated.

1. Preparing and designing the fabric.
2. The wax and how to apply it.
3. The dyes, overdyeing, and crackling.
4. Removing the wax and fixing the color.

After you are familiar with how the batik process develops, consult chapter 3 for additional working methods, types of fabrics, various resist materials, and ways to apply them using tjantings and tjaps (Javanese tools with modern improvisations), and special effects. Teaching batik has proved that the simpler it is at the onset, the more fun it is to progress to different ways of handling the medium.

1. PREPARING AND DESIGNING THE FABRIC

You can begin with fabric you probably have. Use a good size rectangle or square of old sheet that has been washed several times. Be sure it is not too worn or it will tear from the pulling necessary to keep it stretched on a

MATERIALS:
Clockwise: frame, thumbtacks, pencil, paintbrushes, piece of washed 100 percent cotton fabric, wax with pan and heating device, rubber gloves, plastic or enamel vessels for dyeing, paper towels, iron, dyes, salt, thermometer, and stirring spoons. For dyeing, wear an apron.

frame. Or buy a yard of 100 percent cotton or muslin or linen. (*Do not* buy synthetic fabrics or any with permanent-press finishes; they will not dye well.) All new fabrics *must* be washed with hot soapy water, rinsed and dried; this removes factory-applied sizing and starch, which retard dye penetration.

Draw the design on the fabric with a pencil, ball-point pen, or charcoal. Batik requires a different thought approach to design than does printing or drawing. When you draw you add the dark shapes against a light background. In batik, you retain the light shapes with wax and add the dark areas as you dye. It is almost learning to think negatively. By doing a few batiks you will get the feel of how this works. You can also wax directly without a preliminary drawing.

Stretch the fabric fairly taut over an old picture frame, a cardboard box, or special batik frame (see page 30). Keeping the fabric above the work surface assures more complete wax penetration.

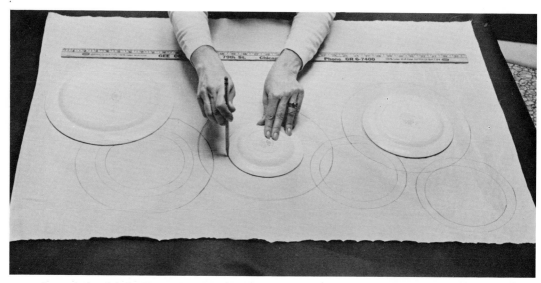

Spread the fabric flat and lightly draw the design with pencil, pen, or charcoal. You can place a paper sketch beneath the fabric and trace it. You can also wax directly on the fabric without a sketch. Circles are easily made with different size plates. Fabric must be pre-washed and dried. It must not be a synthetic fabric or have permapress or soil-resistant finish. A long ruler helps make straight lines. Small details can be developed by drawing with the wax as you work.

Tack the fabric to the frame so it is taut. If it is bigger than the frame, wax one portion, then move the material over to complete the waxing. For other frames, see pages 48-50.

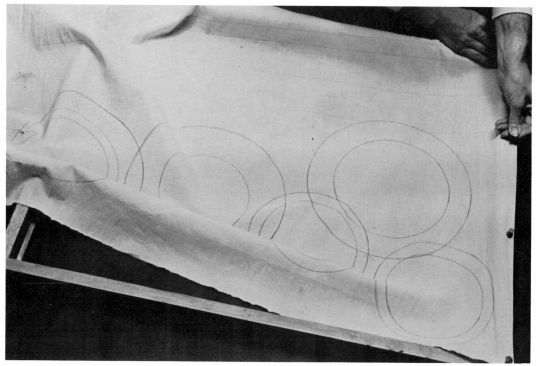

2. THE WAX AND HOW TO APPLY IT

Wax is the resist material: it must be melted and applied to the fabric with a brush. Paraffin wax used to seal Mason jars is available at the grocery store. A mixture of about 50–50 paraffin and beeswax is easiest to work with, but 100 percent paraffin can be used. Beeswax is available from craft shops, art suppliers, and some bee farms. A higher concentration of paraffin will result in more crackle because it is more brittle than beeswax.

Melt the wax in a double boiler on the stove or on a hot plate that has a thermostat control or in an old electric frypan. It can be melted in a pan set on an asbestos pad over the heat source. When the wax is too hot and begins to smoke, turn it down. Wax at the proper temperature will penetrate the fabric and have a translucent appearance. If it is too cool it will be white and opaque and not penetrate the fabric, resulting in only a partial resist. If this occurs, rewax the fabric from the other side. Never leave hot wax unattended; wax fires can be dangerous. Keep baking soda handy and, in case of a wax fire, douse the flames with the dry soda. Never use water.

Apply the wax with soft, inexpensive, natural-bristle paintbrushes of different widths, artists' brushes, or paste brushes. Once brushes are used for wax they are not good for anything else, so the least expensive brushes you can find are adequate. Put the brush in the wax to let it get hot. Eliminate excess wax from the brush by touching the brush to the side of the pan. As you transfer the wax from pan to fabric it may drip where you don't want it to. A folded piece of newspaper, a plastic cup, or jar lid held beneath the brush will catch accidental drippings.

Try *not* to cover your design outlines with wax or these will appear in the white areas. Wax about an $\frac{1}{8}$ inch from the line so that the line will be dyed in darker colors. If the hot wax tends to overshoot the line, place the loaded wax brush away from the line and let the wax spread until you get the feel of it. You can brush water on the line to dampen it and repel the wax.

First waxing: wax only those areas that you want to remain white. For this batik, pink, bright red, and navy blue will be used. The circles are waxed and will be white. In the first dipping, all unwaxed areas will dye pink. Place the brush between the lines and let the wax flow toward the line trying not to cover the line. If the line is waxed it will be in the white part of the fabric. (This is not a disaster because it will be lost among the crackles or removed when dry cleaned.)

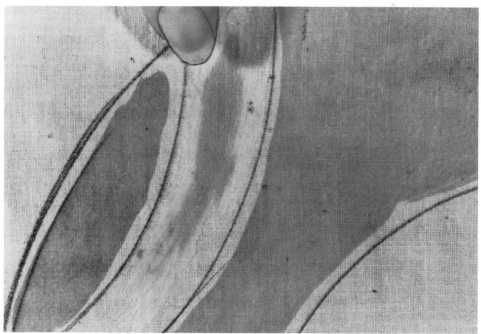

Wax must be applied hot enough so it is translucent as seen in the dark areas. The opaque, white areas show where the wax has not penetrated the fabric; it will not resist the dye color in that area.

Check the back of the fabric and rewax any opaque white areas from the back. Holding the fabric up to the light will reveal any unwaxed areas quickly.

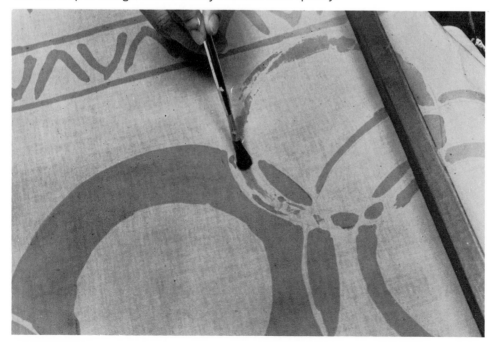

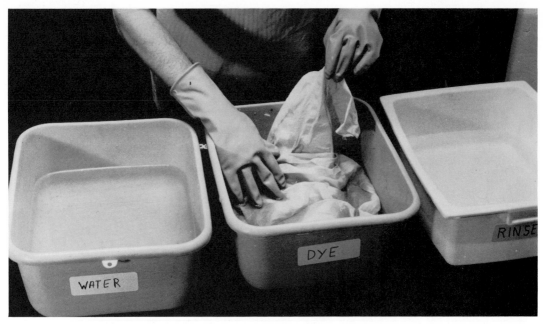

Soaking and dyeing can be done in laundry tubs or sinks or in plastic, enamel, or glass vessels. Wear an apron and rubber gloves. Soak the waxed fabric in cool water for 3 to 5 minutes. The larger the dye vessel, the less the material will have to be crushed. Place material in the dye vessel with enough liquid to cover the material completely. After dyeing, rinse off excess dye.

3. DYES AND DYEING PROCEDURES

Special cold water batik dyes are best and are available from your craft supplier or from sources listed in the back of the book. All purpose household dyes such as Rit, Putnam, Cushing, and Tintex will yield satisfactory results. Household dyes are meant to be used in simmering hot water dyebaths for best colors. *For batik, hot dyebaths cannot be used or the wax will melt.* Therefore you must alter the package instructions. Dissolve the dye in a small amount of hot water, shaking it in a bottle or stirring it until it is dissolved; pour the dye into the cooler water in the dye vessel. A good temperature is 90° to 100°, which is just below the melting point of wax. The higher the temperature at which these dyes are used, the better the color, so don't make solutions ice cold. Do follow instructions about adding salt; its function is to help the dye molecules enter the fibers.

For your first project select two shades of one color for the first two dyebaths and a dark color for the third. For example:

> pink, red, and navy blue
> light blue, royal blue, navy blue
> tan, chestnut brown, black
> light green, dark green, black

Dye vessels should be enamel, stainless steel, plastic, or glass and large enough to move the material about freely. Use pails, dishpans, sinks, children's plastic swimming pools, sandboxes, or baby bathtubs. The dyebath should have enough liquid to cover the fabric.

The waxed fabric is first placed in cool water for three to five minutes to moisten all fibers uniformly preparatory to dyeing; it also helps harden the

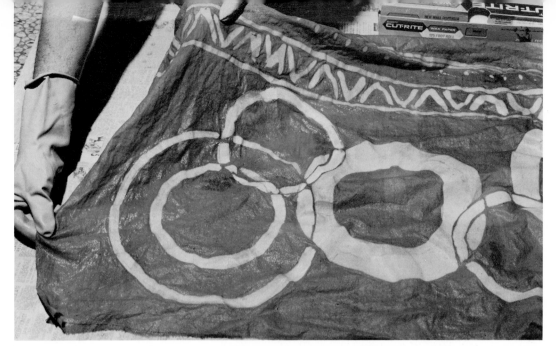

Lay fabric out to dry on newspaper covered with wax paper or plastic. Do not hang to dry. To avoid any inks transferring to the fabric, do not place directly on newsprint.

wax. During the soaking try not to bend the waxed areas so they will remain white; cracks in the wax permit color to seep in.

Then move the fabric into the dyebath. The longer the cloth stays in the dyebath, the stronger the color. Color tint is also controlled by the amount of dye used in relation to the size of the material. Use a test strip of fabric to check the color. Colors always look darker when they are wet than when they are dry.

Remove the fabric from the dye and rinse in cool water. Spread the fabric out on wax paper or plastic to dry. Hanging is not recommended because the colors can run down, resulting in a darker shade at the bottom than at the top of the fabric. Clotheslines sometimes absorb dye from the fabric and leave a streak.

REWAXING AND OVERDYEING

Now all unwaxed areas will have your first color. Put the fabric on the frame again. The second waxing will cover all areas that will remain pink. They appear dark here because of the translucence of the wax. Soaking and dyeing procedures are repeated for the second color, which is bright red.

The third waxing covers all red areas that will remain red, leaving some of the red to be overdyed with the final color, navy blue. These unwaxed red areas will turn purple because navy mixed with red yields purple.

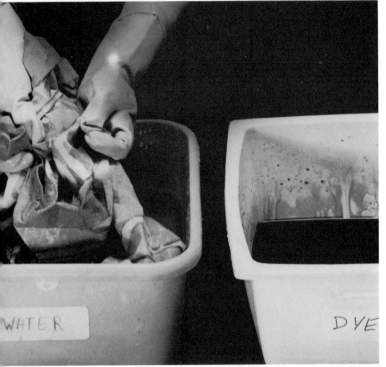

CRACKLING

Put the fabric in cold water to harden the wax thoroughly. (It can be placed in a refrigerator for an hour or so for greater crackle.) Crush the fabric before and while it is in the water. Then place it in the dyebath and stir. With experience, you'll learn how much crushing to do for the amount of crackle you want in a specific piece. (*Note:* Crackle in earlier colors can be achieved by this process. To hold the lighter color crackle, simply wax over the area before redyeing.)

4. REMOVING THE WAX AND FIXING THE COLOR

Use an ironing board, or a larger work surface to minimize moving the fabric about. Pad the surface with newspapers, then sandwich the fabric between paper towels.

Iron over the top layer of paper with a hot iron. This pulls the wax out of the fabric and into the papers. Change the papers top and bottom frequently while ironing. The heat of the iron is usually sufficient to set colors. Sometimes dark wax rings remain. To avoid this, cover the dark colors with wax before ironing.

Any residual wax can be removed by soaking the fabric in a cleaning fluid, such as carbon tetrachloride, or white gasoline. Always work out of doors and do not rub fabric. It can be sent to the cleaner or put in a dry cleaning machine. If boilproof dyes are used, the fabric can be put in boiling water for a few minutes. Add cold water to solidify wax, move wax aside and lift out fabric. Do not throw wax down drains. Some wax left in wall hangings gives them more body, makes them more translucent and dust protected. Follow specific dye instructions for additional washing and fixing procedures.

The finished batik. Dona Meilach.

Another idea for creating design is to cut out a letter from the alphabet in different sizes and styles and overlay and trace them on the fabric. This batik will be pink, purple, and black on white muslin. The fabric is washed and dried. The background is waxed, being careful not to cover the drawn lines.

Notice the difference in the application of wax. The whitish area indicates that the wax has not penetrated the fabric; the darker area is where it has penetrated. Where the wax has not penetrated the fabric, turn the frame over, hold the fabric above your work surface and rewax from the back.

All the background has been waxed to keep it white; a tiny amount of crackle will appear pink where the wax has cracked. In the first dyebath, all the D shapes will be pink.

It is rewaxed where the pink is to be held. Next all unwaxed shapes will be dyed purple; then the purple areas rewaxed. Only those areas to be dyed black will remain unwaxed.

The finished batik, pink, purple, and black. Dona Meilach. 44 inches high, 18 inches wide.

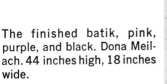

HANGING.   Laverne Leroy. 38 inches high, 27 inches wide. Dark blue on white. An effective color scheme using one dyebath. Only the white areas were waxed and then the fabric dipped in dark blue.

Courtesy, artist

INDIAN PATTERNS.   Eva Birkner. 62 inches high, 18 inches wide. The entire background was partially waxed (the figures unwaxed) and dipped first in a light gold, then rewaxed and dyed a chestnut brown. The background was then thoroughly waxed and crackled. Only the Indian designs remained unwaxed so they would be the final darkest color of dark bronze that also filled in the crackle.

Courtesy, artist

FABRIC LENGTH.   Gloria Perrino. 2½ yards by 48-inch width. White with navy blue.

Courtesy, artist

PROUD PEACOCKS.   Esther Robinson. 48 inches high, 40 inches wide. Black and white "discharge" dye. Begin with black fabric, wax the areas you wish to keep black. Place the fabric in color remover to achieve the white shapes.

INDIAN MOTHER WITH PAPOOSE. Ethyl Wirtshafter. 23 inches high, 18 inches wide. White, gray, red, and brown. Only the white outlines were first waxed, then the fabric dipped in light gray. The gray areas were waxed and the fabric then dipped in red. The majority of the background is red. Portions of red were waxed, leaving all areas to be black unwaxed, including the dark border, the hair shapes, and the crackle.

SUGAR PLUM TREE. Blanche Carstenson. China silk wall hanging on cotton. 38 inches high, 26 inches wide. Repeat circles created by using the edge of an orange juice can as a tjap . . . the can edge is dipped in wax and the wax is stamped onto the fabric.

3

MORE WORKING METHODS AND MATERIALS

THERE is no one best way to do batik, no one best fabric or class of dye to use. Preferences and results are as varied as the artists themselves. After you have created one or two batiks, you will be ready to seek additional ways to work, fabrics, tools for applying waxes, wax combinations, and a multitude of possible variations. Some methods are better suited for specific working situations. Schools, for example, rarely have budgets to buy wooden frames or space to store them, so students learn to work with the fabric in their hands or over newspapers. Cold resin resists may be more practical for certain applications.

The working procedures illustrated in this chapter were taken in actual situations. The setups may help you utilize the space you have more efficiently whether it is in your home or in a classroom.

One procedure especially warrants emphasis because it was most frequently recommended but most often neglected. *Keep an extra strip of fabric for testing colors before immersing an entire piece in dye.* The strip can also serve as a control for determining how boiling, washing, and light will affect the material. Refer to chapter 14 for complete dye information.

FABRICS

For best results, use only natural fibers, not synthetic, for batik and tie-dye. Natural fibers include cotton, linen, silk, and wool. Cotton and linen come from plants, silk from the cocoon of the silkworm, and wool from sheep. Varieties of fabric made with these fibers include mercerized and unmercerized cotton, muslin, batiste, percale, cotton velveteen, corduroy, suede cloth, duck, canvas, pure linens, silks, silk brocades, and wools. Burlap, made from jute and hemp plants, can be dyed also. Silk has a wonderful shimmering quality. Heavy fabrics and those with a nap pose some problem with waxing and wax removal but the appearance of the dye on a nap fabric is lovely. Always iron fabrics with a nap from the back.

Synthetic, or man-made, fibers include Dacron, nylon, rayon acrylics, polyesters, and their blends. They do not take dye well. Some household dyes are blended to dye synthetics, but the results are neither strong nor permanent for batik and tie-dye and hardly worth the effort. Only viscose rayon can be used successfully for dyeing.

All commercial fabrics are produced with a starch or sizing. This sizing prevents dye penetration. *Always wash new materials in hot water with soap or detergents.* Fabrics with heavy sizing may require two or three washings. A capful of water softener (Calgon) will make the fabric more receptive to even dyeing. Wool should be washed in warm 100° water to prevent shrinkage and handled gently to prevent matting. Unsized fabrics are available from sources listed in the appendix.

Any soil-repellent finishes on a fabric must be removed before dyeing can be accomplished. (Perma-press—a permanent resin coating—cannot be used and fabrics with this label must be rejected.) Simmer fabric for 30 minutes in 190° water to which ½ ounce of muriatic acid per 2 gallons of water has been added. Rinse thoroughly and wash in detergent to remove the acid. Fabrics used for tie-dye may be mordanted (soaked in a special solution that makes the fibers absorb the dye better). See mordanting recipes, pages 266–267.

Loosely woven fabrics should be stitched along the edges before washing to prevent fraying and raveling. Colored materials require prewashing also. When discharge methods are planned, pretest a sample of the fabric in different bleach solution proportions (page 265). When you shop for fabrics, carry a small bottle of bleach and buy a strip or ask the salesperson to tear off a piece of fabric. Dip it in the bleach to see if color discharge is satisfactory.

BURN TEST FOR FABRICS

You can test the content of fabric by a "burn" test. When a match is placed to a piece of cotton, viscose rayon, or linen, the smell will resemble burning paper and the piece will flame and form gray ashes. Silk and wool will burn and smell like burning hair or feathers and will form soft black ashes. Synthetic fabrics such as acetates, acrylics, nylons, and polyesters, when burned, will emit a chemical odor; they melt and form a hard bead or lump when cool. They will flame.

SILK HANGING.   Pat Obye. Batik on silk moiré. 60 inches high, 40 inches wide. The watermarks of the moiré add textural interest to the batik. The fabric was so sheer and delicate that it was lost against a wall so the artist added a free-hanging lining of silk behind it.

HANGING *(detail).*   Hallie Redman. Burlap, a natural fabric made from jute, offers a different, rougher texture than silk. It is harder to work with because the waxes do not penetrate as readily. A combination of dyeing and discharge was used. The bleach ate through some of the fibers so Mrs. Redman purposely opened and frayed these and other areas to create negative spaces.

FRAMES AND OTHER METHODS FOR HOLDING FABRICS

Adjustable wood frames especially made for batik are convenient and versatile. They are adjustable to any size cloth within the overall dimension of the frame so that you can work on squares and narrow and wide rectangles. They are simply four strips of wood grooved so the strips fit into one another as shown.

Frames can be purchased ready-made from batik supply dealers, they can be ordered to size from a woodworker or lumber supplier, or made in a home workshop. The smaller frame shown is made from four lengths of 23″ × 1″ × 1″ pine (which are actually ¾″ × ¾″ × ¾″). A groove ¾ inch wide × ⅜ inch deep is made every 2¼ inches. There are 7 grooves on each board.

The larger frame is made from four lengths of 40″ × 3¾″ × 1″ pine. Each groove is ¾ inch wide by 1⅝ inches deep and spaced 2⅛ inches apart. There are 13 grooves. For best results, line up all four boards and put them through the router simultaneously. Larger frames may require a central crossbar to prevent the waxed fabric from sagging.

If the frame is larger than the worktable and the boards tend to come apart, tie them together or use C-clamps at the corners to hold them. Then pin or wax the fabric to the frame.

Artists' stretcher bars assembled for frames can be used. Boxes and assorted picture frames of any size are easily adapted. Any device will work so long as it keeps the fabric taut and above the table allowing the wax to penetrate the material completely.

A cardboard box with the top cut away can be used as a frame. If the box is small, wax part of the fabric and then move it up.

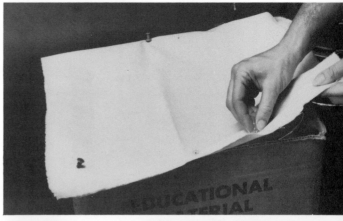

You can pin the fabric to a wall or wallboard, then tape it or weight it at the bottom to keep it taut.

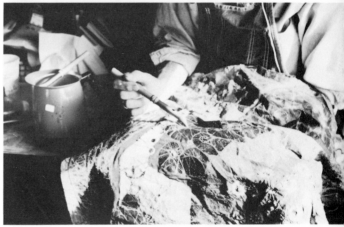

Stephen Blumrich holds the fabric over the palm of his hand. In many schools, the work surface is newspapers and the areas of fabric being waxed are held away from the table by the free hand. (See page 51.)

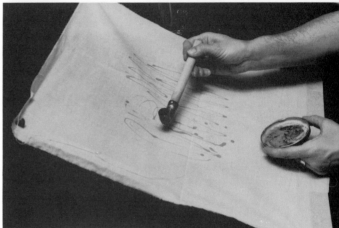

For large pieces use long boards and clamp the corners with C-clamps. Frames can be supported over two sawhorses, the backs of two chairs, on or between two tables. A central support lath may be necessary.

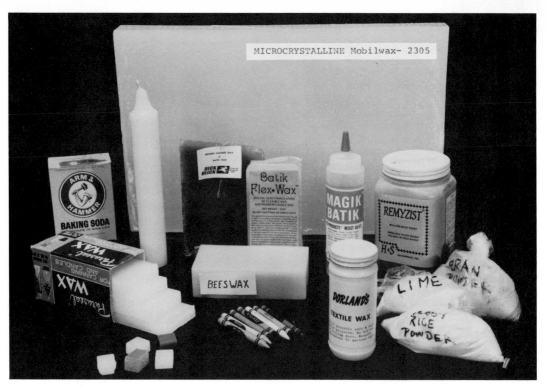

Types of waxes, resins, and paste ingredients and other resists used in batik are described below.

WAXES, OTHER RESISTS, AND HOW TO USE THEM

In chapter 2, paraffin was recommended for the resist medium because it was readily available. Combinations of paraffin with beeswax yield various degrees of crackle. Paraffin is brittle and cracks readily so the more paraffin in a mixture, the greater the crackle. Beeswax is flexible and bends without crackling so the more beeswax, the less crackle. A mixture of 50–50 paraffin and beeswax is most often used; other proportions should be tested for individual preferences.

Candle wax is usually a pure, hard paraffin and can be used. Microcrystalline Mobilwax® #2305 comes in large slabs often used for sculpting. It is a mixture of five kinds of paraffin and is flexible and less expensive than beeswax. Many companies are premixing beeswax and paraffin in one cake and marketing it as batik wax. Crayola crayons and colored candle waxes can be used for colored wax batik described in chapter 8. The washing soda used to set fiber reactive dyes often eats through the beeswax after two or three dippings, so fabrics should be rewaxed when several overdyes are planned.

Cold resin resists for use with hot dyeing are relatively new. They are applied to the fabric in a liquid and allowed to dry. They remain solid when placed in the hot dye solution and can be simmered for use with household dyes. They are washed out with cold water. Resin resists are applied with a brush, spatula, or from squeeze bottles with different size openings. Their advantages are that you do not have the potential hazard of hot wax which many school systems frown upon. They can be used with inexpensive household dyes. They are very flexible and will not produce a crackle when a plain resist is desirable.

Eleanor Levine works with two electric frypans: one pan holds 1 part paraffin to 3 parts microcrystalline wax and is applied to areas where she does not want crackle; the other pan holds 3 parts paraffin and 1 part microcrystalline wax for areas where she does want crackle.

Courtesy, artist

Wax can be heated in a double boiler on the stove.

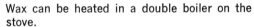

Several cans of wax set in hot water on a hot plate work well for classroom setup. Students can move the cans to their work; they should use potholders.

Photographed at Avila College, Kansas City, Mo.

Electric corn poppers placed on fireproof asbestos pads are handy for melting wax. Different proportions are used in each of these pots for controlling crackle. Notice that the artist works holding the fabric up and without using a frame.

Photographed at Northern Illinois University, DeKalb

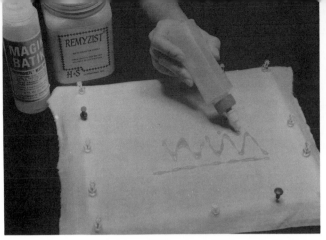

Cold resin resists are applied to the fabric as a clear liquid. The fabric should be dried flat, preferably on absorbent paper. If it is handled while wet, the resin on the fabric may stick to itself.

The fabric should be placed into a hot dye or bleach bath at least 125°, where the resin solidifies and turns white.

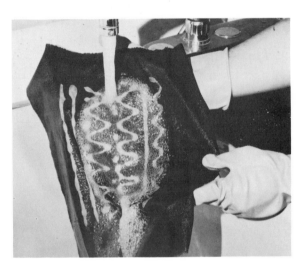

To rinse, first run under hot water to remove excess dye or bleach. Then place under cold running water for about 15 minutes and rub the fabric to remove the resist. Or let the resin resist remain and apply another coat of resist to retain some of the color, then redye. Wax may also be used after the resins are rinsed out. But if wax is used first, it must be removed before using the resin resists or it will melt in hot dye.

Dorland's Textile Wax can be applied cold also, but it cannot be used for dipping unless it is applied to both sides of the fabric. It is recommended for direct dye application described in chapter 6. The same is true for starch-paste resists.

Vegetable shortenings such as Crisco and Mazola oil are also effective resists in cold water dyeing, for direct dye application and for discharge dyeing on some fabrics. Thick shortenings such as Crisco can be applied with serrated-edge blades for textures, with spatulas, brushes, fingers, or squeeze tubes used for starch resist (page 122). Always pretest the resist and its effectiveness before working on an entire piece of fabric.

Many different effects can be developed by variations in applying the resists and the following are some suggestions with melted wax.

1. Soft edges with a slight bleeding can be obtained by melting the edge of the wax along the line you want to soften. Use an old iron kept for this purpose or a spatula held over the heat and then quickly placed at the edge of the wax. The dye then seeps in around the edges.

2. For subtle shading wax only the back of the fabric rather than penetrating it. After a first dyebath, wax the fabric back and front and

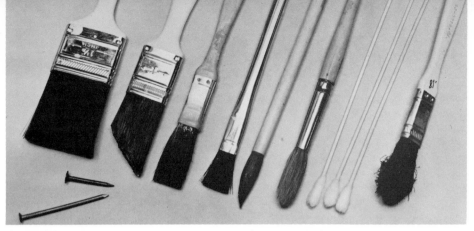

Brushes for applying wax are, preferably, natural bristle, assorted sizes, and inexpensive. An angled brush can be made from a straight brush and is convenient for waxing close to lines. Dip a brush in wax and then cut the bristles on the angle desired. Oriental ink brushes can be worked to a fine point for drawing lines with wax or working close to lines. Nails, toothpicks, and dental instruments are used for scratching lines in wax. Do not let bristles rest on the bottom of the hot pan or they will become misshapen and unusable, as shown in the brush, right. Nylon bristles tend to frizz up when they get hot.

An applicator for waxing broad areas and creating an interesting texture can be made by rolling a length of burlap, about 4 inches wide, over a dowel rod and wrapping it tightly. Dip the rolled end in the wax. When wax is applied to the fabric with this "brush," scratchy textures result.

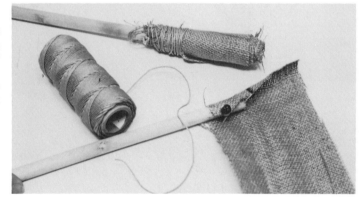

the result will be a halftone of the dye shade.

3. Dip the waxed fabric in dye that is warm enough to melt the wax slightly for an interesting bubble-like texture. Or, after waxing, place the fabric in the sun or in a hot car in the summer so it melts uniformly; then dip in dye. Of course, if you don't want it to melt, avoid keeping the waxed fabric in a closed car during the hot summer.

4. Scratch through the wax with a nail, toothpick, or dental pick to create many kinds of linear effects from a single line to cross-hatching. Be careful not to go through the fabric.

5. Sometimes a dark wax line remains after the wax is ironed out. This line can enrich the surface by supplying an extra dark outline area and can be planned as part of the design.

Never leave hot wax unattended. This is a basic safety precaution. Should a wax fire occur in the pot, place a lid over the pot to smother the fire. If fire begins from wax spilled on the burner, turn off the heat and douse with dry baking soda. A tri-class fire extinguisher will also put out wax fires. If hot wax is spilled on the skin, immerse the burned area in cool water and see a physician.

LAMENT.   Arnelle A. Dow. Batik on cotton duck. 20½ inches high, 22 inches wide. A minimum amount of crackling appears in the finished batik.

Courtesy, artist

CRACKLE EFFECTS

The characteristic crackle of batik can be greatly varied. It can range from an absence of the veining to a thorough and heavily crackled appearance. For crisp, clean crackle lines, place the waxed fabric in a refrigerator or freezer for about an hour before crackling. Wet out the fabric in cold water and bend and crush the wax. Stir frequently while the material is in the dyebath.

The direction of the crackle can be controlled by carefully folding the fabric vertically, diagonally, or horizontally. Jerome Wallace makes accordion folds that radiate from the center of a piece.

Portions of a batik can be crackled by varying the type and proportions of wax (already mentioned under waxes). Resins can be used for eliminating crackle in hot dyeing. You can also control crackled areas by applying dyes with a brush rather than dipping. After crushing the fabric, brush on dye only over the areas where you want crackle. Rewax any areas you do not want to crackle and place in dyebath, if necessary, to complete the final dyeing for dark outlines and/or shapes.

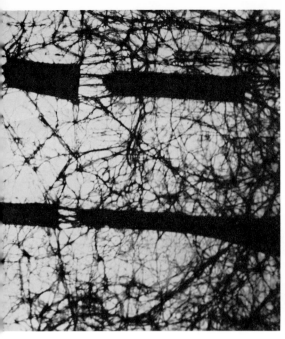

AMOR (detail). Enza Quargnali. 84 inches by 84 inches. Overall heavy veining, or crackle, can be achieved by placing the waxed fabric in the freezer before cracking and by stirring the batik frequently and thoroughly while it is in the final dyebath.

Courtesy, artist

BITTERSWEET. Jerome Wallace. By carefully folding the waxed material a controlled radiating design was created in the crackle.

Courtesy, artist

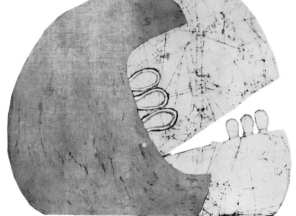

SWALLOWING. Al Meilach. Batik on cotton. The red (left) has minimal crackling; the white (right) is more thoroughly crackled. The materials must be handled carefully and dyed in a large enough container so they do not have to be folded and bent too much.

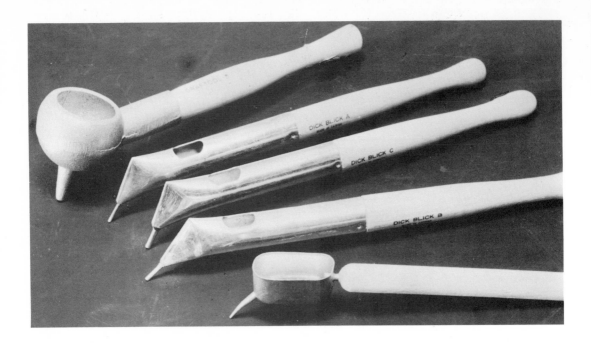

THE TJANTING TOOL

The tjanting tool is used for drawing with hot wax. Those shown (*above*) and in use (*below*) are modern interpretations of an ancient design. Tjantings usually are made of brass or other metal. The cup holds the hot wax which pours out through the spout. Tjantings are made with different size spouts to give different width lines. The tjanting may be held over an alcohol lamp or dipped in the melted wax and carried to the fabric. To prevent the wax from dripping keep a plastic jar lid or folded paper beneath the spout until you are ready to place it on the fabric.

Do not let the tjanting tool remain on the bottom of a pan in which wax is melting; often the heat conducted through the metal melts the solder that holds the spout to the cup.

The cup of the tjanting tool is filled with hot melted wax and carried to the fabric. A plastic jar lid will catch accidental drips and stop the wax flow until you're ready to place it on the fabric.

Lines drawn with the tjanting have a character that cannot be made with a brush. Circles, swirls, curves, dots, and many other motifs are fun to do. Some people work exclusively with the tjanting on an entire batik.

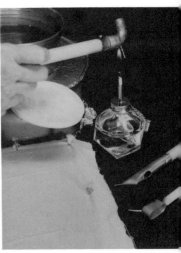

The tjanting may be heated over an alcohol lamp.

WHAT SHAPE IS LONELINESS? Jerome Wallace. 40 in. high, 38 in. wide. Collection, Malcolm McBride, Florence, Italy.
Photo, Robert Goodman

DR. POEL'S PARLOR. Linda Menger. 20 in. high, 15 in. wide. Direct dye application with airbrush on Pellon fabric.
Courtesy, artist

(Top) Batik fabric can be used for upholstery. Jerome Wallace.
Courtesy, artist

(Center) CAFTAN. Judith Jurasik. Batik on muslin. 5½ ft. high.
Courtesy, artist

FRUIT BASKET. Kathleen Knippel. Stuffed batik on Indian Head cotton. Life size.
Courtesy, artist

1. The process of waxing and overdyeing can be seen in this series using white silk. The waxed white areas resist the first yellow dyebath.

2. Some yellow areas were waxed and the piece dyed blue. However, because blue mixed with yellow creates green (see below), the completed color is green.

3. Some green areas were waxed. The piece was crackled and dyed black to result in some solid black areas and black crackle throughout. By Dona Meilach.

The World Book Encyclopedia © 1972
Enterprises Educational Corporation

Red — Yellow
Orange

Yellow — Blue
Green

Blue — Red
Violet

PRIMARY AND SECONDARY COLORS

THE COLOR WHEEL

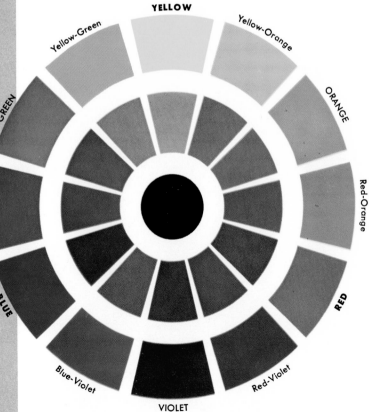

YELLOW
Yellow-Green
Yellow-Orange
GREEN
ORANGE
Blue-Green
Red-Orange
BLUE
RED
Blue-Violet
Red-Violet
VIOLET

The outer circle shows the primary and secondary colors, separated by six intermediate colors. The inner circle shows darker colors obtained by mixing two colors that lie opposite each other in the outer circle.

ASSORTED STUFFED BATIK DOLLS. Candace Johnson. *Courtesy, artist*

SEE ME, FEEL ME, KNOW ME. Eleanor Levine. 46 in. high, 31 in. wide.
Collection, Dr. & Mrs. David McDermid, Calif.

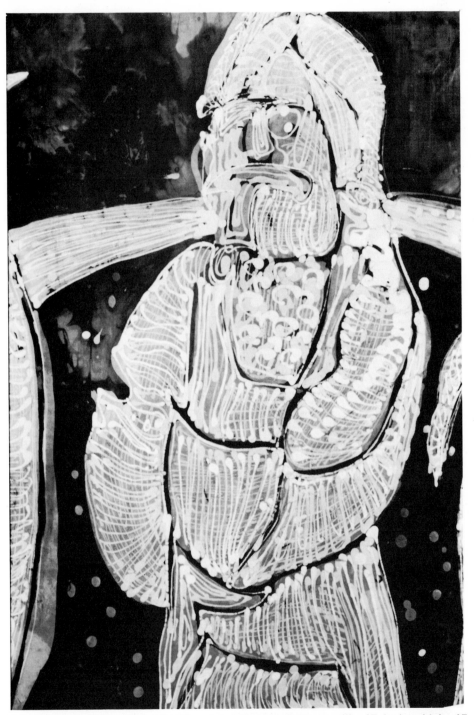

THE PHILOSOPHER KING *(detail)*.   John Mulder: Batik on silk. 47 inches high, 45 inches wide. The tjanting line is a characteristic detail of many batiks. Mr. Mulder's figure is developed almost exclusively with the quick linear quality of a well-controlled tjanting.

A simple homemade tjap is used to stamp repeat patterns with the wax. Directions below.
Courtesy, Bets Ramsey

THE MODERN TJAP—A STAMP FOR WAXING

The intricately patterned traditional Javanese tjap (shown on page 9) used for stamping wax patterns can be simplified and improvised by the craftsman. Easy-to-find stamping items can be employed, including cookie cutters, juice cans, and kitchen utensils such as a potato masher, meat tenderizer, cheese grater, and apple cutter. Found objects can be stamped, such as the head of a hexagon bolt, a key, the edge of a hinge, the rim of a small metal box, a cork, or nails stuck into a block of wood or plastic.

Small metal cutters should be backed with wood or embedded in cork for holding. Metal conducts heat and when it is dipped into wax the item quickly becomes too hot to handle.

You can make a tjap like the one shown with metal stripping used for wrapping cartons, two pieces of wood, plaster of Paris, nails, pliers, and tin shears.

Cut one wood block slightly larger than the size of the metal shape. Nail another smaller wood piece to the back for use as a handle. Bend the metal into the desired shape or shapes remembering that it will print the reverse image on the fabric. Cover the face of the wood block with plaster of Paris mixed moderately thick and build up about 1/4 inch of wet plaster. Set the shaped metal strip into the plaster; place another block of wood on top of the strip to hold it in the plaster and to be sure all surfaces are level. Tie the block together and dry about an hour. When dry, remove the top block and print with the tjap.

To wax, dip the tjap in shallow wax, allow it to heat up, and shake off excess wax before stamping. Work fairly rapidly so metal does not cool.

CHASUBLE. Bets Ramsey. Green voile. Design stamped with tjap *(left)*. The crosses down the front were outlined with a brush around a paper pattern. The fabric was dyed green and the second waxing held back the design. The material was dyed mahogany and blue. It is lined with green.

COUNTRY LIFE. Azis. 24 inches high, 24 inches wide. Tiny dots, circles, scales, and repeat patterns are made with a tjap by the batik folk artist from Djakarta. White with navy blue.
Courtesy, First Editions, San Jose, Calif.

WALL HANGING. June Mayborn Bonner. Cotton. 35 inches high, 57 inches wide. The motif is an old Spanish wrought-iron key used as a wax stamp. Colors are yellow, orange, hot pink, terra-cotta, and a final dye of blue to give the ground a rich chocolate brown while adding a pattern of blue in some of the crackled areas.
Courtesy, artist

KEEPING RECORDS

The first time you try to recreate the color or the effect of an earlier batik, you'll realize the validity of keeping some kind of record for each piece. Record-keeping methods can vary depending upon your method of organization. Many artists suggest keeping a separate strip or an extra strip at the side or top of a piece of fabric that you are batiking. Wax a portion of this extra strip with each dye bath so you'll have a record of how the colors appear. Attach this strip to a card with entries noting the following information:

Title of piece:
Date: Price per yard:
Fabric used: Size and weight of fabric:
Where purchased: Brand of dye used:

	Color and amount	Amount of assistant	Time in dye	Amt. & temp. of water	Color obtained
1st dip					
2nd dip					
3rd dip					

Special procedures and any other comments:

Blanche Carstenson keeps test swatches and dye information in a notebook.

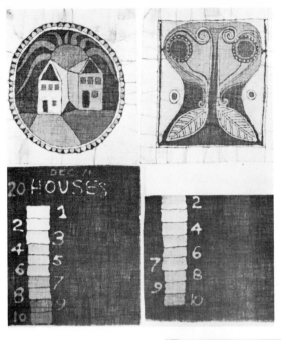

Stephen Blumrich records each dipping and color on a piece of test fabric on which he has waxed the title of the piece, the date, and a square for each successive dyebath.

An accumulation of test fabrics, dyes, waxes used, methods, and comments are hung up in a classroom for quick reference. Blanche Carstenson.

Testing colorfastness and wax removal from boiling off and from steaming in a plastic bag shows the amount of color loss by each method in the two end strips cut from a batik. Dona Meilach.

DUET.   Susan Lobe. Batik on silk. 36 inches high, 30 inches wide. Yellows, blues, blue greens, reds, and black. Primary color combinations achieved by brushing on dyes.

Courtesy, artist

4

COLOR

COLOR is the excitement of batik and tie-dye. Thousands of words can be written about it, but there is no substitute for experiencing the changes that occur in a piece of plain white fabric as it is dipped, then dyed, and overdyed with various hues. The action of the dyes is different from direct painting or printing where you can pretest shades on a palette, put them on the canvas, and scrape them off if you don't like the result. In dyeing there is always the moment when you are not really sure what is going to happen and then, when the colors mix the way you want them to, they seem to sing.

Color is one of the elements of design. An understanding of the basic functions of color will help you use it effectively and with confidence. Three terms are used to describe the characteristics of color: hue, value, and intensity.

HUE refers to basic or pure color. There are several color systems but the easiest and most often used is the PRANG system worked out in the color wheel between pages 72 and 73. In this system three hues—yellow, red, and blue—are called primaries. Three secondary hues and six intermediate hues can be formed by combining each of the primary hues with one of the other two.

When the colors are arranged like the face of a clock in an easy-to-use wheel, the relationships of hues to each other can be seen more readily. Put yellow at 12 o'clock, red at 4 o'clock, and blue at 8 o'clock. By mixing equal parts of each primary hue, the result is a secondary hue. Therefore, yellow mixed equally with red produces orange at the 2 o'clock position. Red mixed equally with blue results in violet at the 6 o'clock position. Blue mixed with yellow makes green at the 10 o'clock position.

The additional six places remaining on the clock are for the third set of colors called intermediate because they lie between the primary and secondary colors. They are made by mixing each hue with its neighbor to result in yellow-orange, red-orange, red-violet, blue-violet, blue-green, and yellow-green.

VALUE refers to the lightness or darkness of a color. If white is added to a color, the result is a tint that is higher in value than the original hue. Pink, for example, is a *tint* of red. If black is added, the value is lowered and that is referred to as a *shade*. Black added to red results in maroon or a lowered shade of red. If both black and white are mixed with a color, the result is called a tone . . . in the case of red, the *tone* would be rose.

INTENSITY is the brightness of a color. This depends on the saturation of a hue in any color mixture. Pure colors are brighter and more intense than color mixed with the neutrals, black, white, or gray. They are more intense than the colors mixed with complementary colors . . . those across from one another on the color wheel.

HOW TO USE THE COLOR WHEEL FOR BATIK AND TIE-DYE

Keeping a color wheel pinned above your dyeing area will help you visualize what will happen when you overdye colors. Dyestuffs and dye classifications do differ but generally you dye the cloth and work your color schemes from light colors to dark. If you dye a first color yellow, for example, and overdye this with blue, the result will be green because yellow mixed with blue becomes green. The same yellow overdyed with red will generally produce orange. Actually, it is difficult to have all three primary colors in one batik created by dipping it, because of the way dyes mix. Fabrics can be waxed to hold areas for other colors, then boiled out and the reserved areas colored next, the first areas waxed. However, all primary colors can be used simultaneously if the dyes are brushed onto the fabric.

If you select any two colors directly opposite each other in the wheel and mix them in equal parts, they will produce a black or dark gray value and they are called complementary colors. When they are mixed together in unequal parts they tend to darken each other. For example, a little blue added to orange, its opposite across the wheel, creates brown; therefore blue dyed over orange will turn the fabric brown. A little orange added to blue will turn the blue a little darker, or slightly green, depending upon the amount added.

There are many possible ways to select a color scheme. *Monochromatic* schemes are one color with various intensities of tints, tones, and shades (Mono= one, chroma=color).

Warm and cool colors can be contrasted. The warm colors on the right side of the wheel, reds, oranges, and yellows, can be alternated with cool colors such as blues and greens much as darks and lights are used to create a sense of balance and unity.

You can also refer to the color wheel to determine the colors that harmonize. These are *complementary* colors that lie directly opposite each other but are not mixed. For example: yellow and violet are complementary and when both appear in a design, they work effectively. By drawing triangles between any three colors, a *harmonizing* scheme can be determined. Draw a triangle from yellow to red-violet and blue-violet for a set of *near-complementary* colors. Color harmony can also be achieved with colors next to each other such as blue and green, red and red-violet, yellow and green, and so on.

Another guide often practiced is to vary the amount of each color in one composition in a 3-2-1 ratio. That is, most of one color, a middle amount of a second color, and the smallest amount of a third color. This rule, often used by painters, is referred to as dominance, subordination, and accent.

Vibrating color schemes result when complementary colors of equal intensity and value are used and juxtaposed. Reds and greens will vibrate when used together.

Limited color combinations can be fun. Select a specific number of colors and limit yourself to using only values of these in a composition.

OTHER SOURCES FOR COLOR SCHEMES

You can hunt for ideas for color combinations in nature and in man-made objects. The colors in a flower can suggest those you can use in a batik. You can even adapt the relationship of color proportionately: a rose for example may be predominantly red, with tints and tones of pink, and dark accents in the center. You can use this same distribution of color in a wall hanging that may have no relationship to a rose.

Wallpapers, printed fabrics, and interior decorating can inspire color relationships. Observe how the colors in a TV picture relate; think of a person's clothes and the background used and how these colors can be applied to a foreground image and background in a batik. The jagged lines on an imperfect color TV image are marvelous sources for color inspiration and linear patterns.

It is wise to preplan a color scheme by sketching it on paper or blackboard to determine where you want which colors. Dye colors and relationships can be simulated with colored pencils, watercolors, waterproof inks, felt-tip pens, or chalk. Then use the design as a guide when you wax the fabric.

MIXING DYES BEFORE DIPPING

At first, you'll be intrigued with how colors mix during the overdyeing process. As you progress, you may want to mix colors *before* they are put into the dyebath. In most dyes, the color range is limited so mixing becomes essential. The color wheel is your guide to color mixing. The amount of color used will depend on the value desired in relation to the weight of the materials. (See chapter 14.)

Colors can be mixed using any of the following three procedures, depending upon the degree of accuracy and care you want to exercise.

1. Mix the dye powder, carefully measuring in teaspoons or ounces the amount of dye used for a specific mixture if you hope to duplicate the color.
2. Mix equal amounts of dyestuff, then paste and dissolve each in one cup of warm water. Then mix the dissolved dyes in the ratio desired: for example, mix yellow and blue equally, each in one cup of water. Then use ¾ cup yellow to ¼ cup blue for a light green.
3. Mix colors in the dye bath by eye and by dipping test fabric strips to test value. Remember, the longer the fabric is in the dye, the darker it gets. This is not accurate or measurable, but works for one-time projects.

To obtain major colors use the following ratios:

red	100%	red
red-orange	¾	red–¼ yellow
orange	½	red–½ yellow
yellow-orange	¼	red–¾ yellow
yellow	100%	yellow
yellow-green	¾	yellow–¼ blue
green	½	yellow–½ blue
green-blue	¼	yellow–¾ blue
blue	100%	blue
blue-violet	¾	blue–¼ red
violet	½	blue–½ red
red-violet	¼	blue–¾ red

The original color (unless white or off-white) will always affect the color you are dyeing. Dark dye shades of red, blue, green, etc., will usually cover light shades of other colors.

To dye fabric black:

Over green, brown, or yellow, use one part navy blue for each two or three parts black.

Over red or purple, use one part forest green or olive green for each two or three parts black.

Over blue, use one part orange for each part black.

If too much black is used, material may have a brownish cast.

COLOR CHART FOR OVERDYEING

Note: Colors vary by distributors. Color charts are available. Generally, mixing and overdyeing primary and secondary colors in any dye class will yield colors close to those listed.

COLOR CHART FOR OVERDYEING

DYE COLOR	OVER RED PRODUCES	OVER YELLOW PRODUCES	OVER BROWN PRODUCES	OVER ORANGE PRODUCES	OVER GREEN PRODUCES	OVER PURPLE PRODUCES	OVER BLUE PRODUCES
Red	Darker Red	Scarlet	Reddish Brown	Light Red	Dull Brown	Reddish Purple	Purple
Blue	Purple	Green	Very Dark Brown	Dull Dark Gray	Bottle Green	Bluish Purple	Deep Blue
Yellow	Scarlet	Deep Yellow	Golden Brown	Yellow Orange	Light Green	Greenish Brown	Green
Brown	Brownish Red	Yellowish Brown	Darker Brown	Yellowish Dark Brown	Greenish Brown	Chocolate	Almost Black
Orange	Red	Light Orange	Tobacco Brown	Deep Orange	Yellowish Green	Reddish Brown	Dull Dark Gray
Green	Almost Black	Light Green	Olive Drab	Myrtle Green	Darker Green	Dull Dark Gray	Greenish Blue
Purple	Reddish Purple	Almost Black	Very Dark Reddish Brown	Light Dull Purple	Dull Dark Purple	Darker Purple	Plum

EXAMPLE: Pink over Light Blue   produces Lavender
             Pink over Light Yellow   produces Shell Pink
             Pink over Light Orange   produces Coral Pink

Chart, Courtesy Putnam Dyes, Inc.
Quincy, Ill. 62307

5

DESIGN IDEAS AND INSPIRATION

AFTER you are familiar with the techniques of batik and how colors react from resists and overdyes, you can concentrate on creating designs. To some people the expanse of fabric to be filled is a challenge. They quickly sketch in areas that relate to one another and are rhythmic and pleasing. These people have a feeling for design. To others, the empty canvas is a yawning chasm and they must struggle with an answer to What shall I draw? How do I create a design? What shall I use for motifs? How should the parts be arranged?

Trained artists learn to discover design ideas almost everywhere they look. They know what to look for and how to translate what they see into designs. But everyone can train himself to look and see as the artist sees. A good beginning is to observe objects in terms of the design elements: *line, shape, space, texture,* and *color.*

The artist looks for shapes that are interesting in themselves and in relation to other shapes. He may remember these shapes as forms that have line around them to define them, or as composed of lines that give them form. A tree, for example, has a shape that can be outlined and made up of lines. So the artist thinks about how he will portray that shape with line.

Line has movement . . . the tree can be drawn still or swaying, heavy or thin, depending upon how the line is used; it can be strong and upright using bold, straight lines; or it can suggest a different character if it is drawn with wiggly thin lines. So, the first lesson is to learn to observe line by itself and in relation to shape.

Shape is all around you from the period at the end of this sentence, to the shape of the page, to the shape of the world itself. Everything has shape; some shapes are more interesting than others. A sand-smoothed pebble may have an amoeboid shape; the sheet of paper you are reading has a rectangular shape. How can you use these shapes in design? You learn to relate them in *space* to other shapes. In batik, the fabric is the space that must contain related shapes. You could use the rectangular page and the pebble to begin a design.

◄

PACIFICA.   Jack Lenor Larsen. A feeling of stylized waves is based on a repeat pattern of diamond shapes with rhythmic, varying lengths and widths of lines moving in opposing directions. Small circles and swirls lend to the overall feeling of movement.

Courtesy, Larsen Design Studio, New York

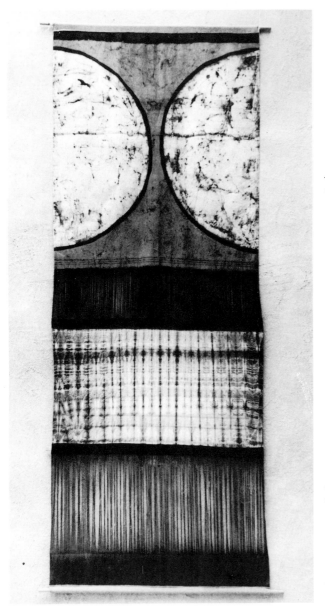

THERE ARE TWO SIDES TO EVERYTHING.
Beth Ford. Tie-dye and batik on cotton
muslin with large open areas bordered in
black felt. Purple and black on white
silk. 108 inches high, 40 inches wide. A
symmetrical design based on the circle
and rectangle.

Courtesy, artist

WE DISSOLVED INTO LIGHT AND
TASTED EACH OTHER. Jerome Wallace.
Multicolored batik. Circles on a rectangular background are contrasted with
stripes, which must really be considered
rectangular shapes of different sizes. The
crackle is controlled so the lines emanate
from the center circle outward.

Courtesy, artist

Place a rectangle on the fabric. Then draw the pebble shape repeated in different sizes and directions. Vary the size of the line that defines the pebble. Add
more rectangles in different sizes and directions: Immediately, you are applying
three elements of design: line, shape, and space.

The next element to consider is *texture*. How will you portray texture
in a tree, in the pebble, or in other objects you draw? The fabric already has
texture, but visual texture may be portrayed by a buildup of tiny dots, or lines,
suggesting smooth and rough surfaces.

After you familiarize yourself with the design elements, think of placing your
objects on the fabric to create a rhythm. Rhythm in an allover pattern is the
result of a repetition of the shapes; often different-sized shapes make a pattern
more interesting than shapes of all one size. Some shapes may be emphasized
more than others by the line around them, the color, the size, or the texture.
Decide whether you want shapes on the space in a symmetrical or asymmetrical

arrangement. If necessary, cut shapes from paper and arrange them on your fabric to determine which relationships to the space and to one another are most interesting.

Designs can be inspired by several sources and the following batiks are grouped to illustrate the application of geometrical shapes, cutout papers, motifs from primitive artifacts, natural and man-made forms, symbolism, and people.

Geometrical Shapes are always a safe and good basis for batik designs. These include circles, squares, diamonds, rectangles, ovals, hexagons, ogees, and scales. Vary their sizes, combine them, use one within another and make rhythmic patterns of them.

Cutout Papers can inspire design. They can be composed of geometrical motifs. They may be simply torn paper shapes distributed on a fabric until they suggest an arrangement. Strips of cut and torn colored art tissue, overlapping one another, can spark both design ideas and color combinations.

TALA. Al Nickel. Batik on linen. 84 inches high, 52 inches wide. The design is a combination of the circle and the square with variations. Colors are white, yellow, red, and purple on a deep blue background. Because linen is a heavy fabric it is often necessary to wax both sides of the material to retain large areas of color.

Courtesy, artist

Motifs from Primitive Artifacts such as masks, furnishings, musical instruments, carved borders, and interior designs are a rich source of ideas that can be found in books, and in natural history and art museums.

Designs *inspired by nature* are popular. Sources are plants, fish-scale colors and patterns, small details of large objects. The seeds and core of an apple can be expanded to become an entire image. Microscopic cutaways of seeds and tissues, biomorphic cell structures are used to inspire total designs. Look for photos of such images in science, medical, and photographic books and magazines.

Man-made Forms in buildings with repeated arches and rectangles, brick arrangements, and decorative sculpture can inspire repeat patterns. Lines and

BLACK AND WHITE. Gloria Perrino. 75 inches high, 34 inches wide. A one-dye-color batik can be extremely dramatic. The composition relies on combinations of several geometric shapes in different sizes: circles, ovals, diamonds, and the resulting negative black areas that remain between them.

Courtesy, artist

negative spaces formed by a bridge superstructure can suggest myriad shapes that can be imposed and superimposed in color when planning a batik. A village with houses crawling up a hillside can be designed as variations of overlapping rectangles of different sizes and shapes. See page 143.

Symbolism is a marvelous ploy used by artists to portray personal ideas. A line from a poem, the title of a play, the imagery evoked from reading a passage in a novel are all ideas for stimulating subjects and designs. Many people use doodles and develop them into abstract drawings.

One pitfall of batik is that the colors often are so magnificent that they overshadow the design itself. But a truly successful piece must be a combination of good color, good design, and good craftsmanship.

BLUE MEDALLIONS.   Jennifer Lew. Batik on China silk. 15 inches high, 18 inches wide. More interpretations of circles within circles combined with lines and abstract petal shapes which are parts of ovals or scales.

Courtesy, American Craftsmen's Council

►

PRIMITIVE BULL DRIVER *(border detail).*   Ethyl Wirtshafter. A batik design may require a border to hold the piece together. Border designs can be varied and act as a unifying motif to the composition. Borders should be observed in examples throughout the book. Simple lines, triangles, and elongated pointed ovals with diagonal lines are **effective.**

HANGING *(detail).* Ilona Bodo. The arrangement of geometric shapes can be varied considerably. The half circles are symmetrically arranged along the rectangle with diamonds and circles within.

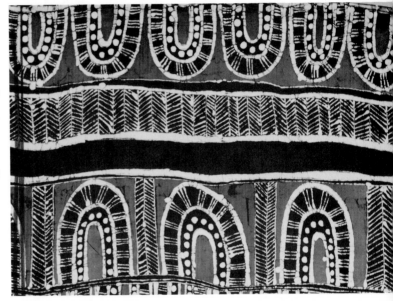

YARDAGE NO. 2 *(detail).* Jennifer Lew. Batik on silk broadcloth. Shapes similar to those used above are varied in size and the base of each half oval or "scale" shape is off-centered from its opposing shape.
Courtesy, American Craftsmen's Council

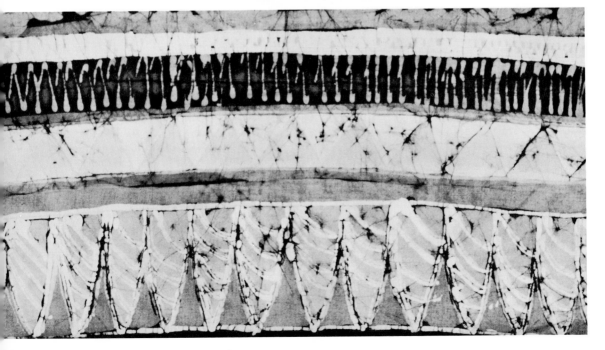

Folded and cut paper shapes can suggest combinations for overall patterns and for symmetrical and asymmetrical designs. Try cutting many shapes and using all or part of the design that pleases you. At bottom right, elements from two cutout patterns have been placed together. Colors were filled in with colored pencil so the artist could translate the design into batik more easily. Hallie Redman.

A paper cutout and the resulting batik in three colors: gray, light blue, and navy blue. Hallie Redman.

A scarf has been designed using shapes suggested from several of the cutouts. It is not necessary to adhere exactly to a cutout. It is merely a tool to use to stimulate ideas when composing designs. Hallie Redman.

Overall repeat patterns were created using a stencil to wax out areas to be resisted. Use a waxed stencil cardboard and, if the wax tends to adhere, dampen the cardboard slightly. In both of these examples, the resist was placed on a dark blue fabric to hold the dark areas; then the fabric was placed in color remover for the discharge dye technique. The result was dark blue patterns on a lighter blue background. Hallie Redman.

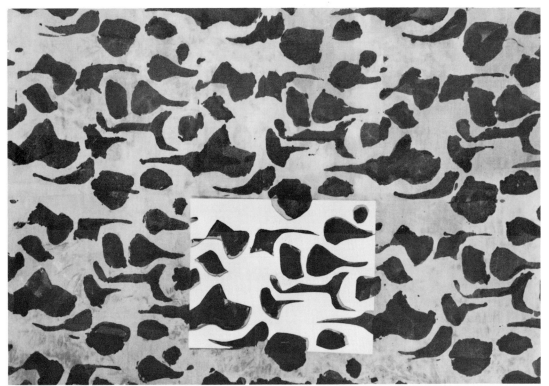

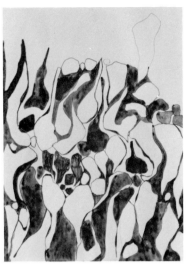

Sketches made in black and white and with colored pencils during otherwise waste-of-time moments by Hallie Redman. These were inspired at the dentist's office and based on tooth shapes.

It's a good idea to keep a notebook with sketches and samples of patterns. Many of these were later applied to larger fabrics. Sometimes a design made on one day and saved will be perfect when new ideas are elusive. Hallie Redman.

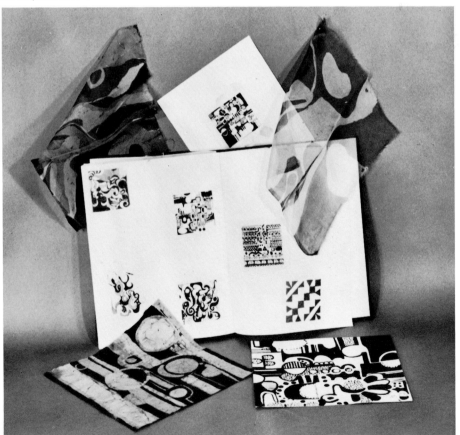

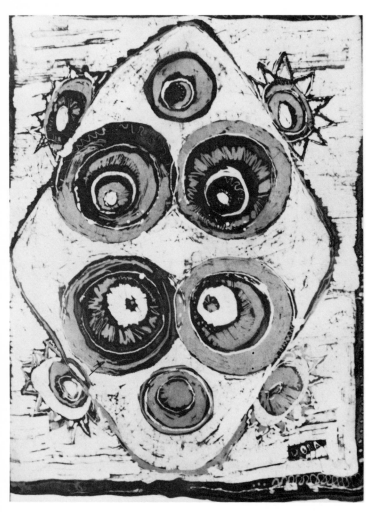

MASK. Dona Meilach. Beige, brown, and black on China silk. 54 inches high, 48 inches wide. Inspiration for and development of the design can be seen below.

A newspaper photo (*below left*) of a mask suggested the design. The top half of the mask was repeated rather than the entire mask. A colored sketch was drawn. White lines around the circles in the finished batik were developed as the waxing progressed. The design was not followed exactly from the drawing.

NEW GUINEA MOTIF.   Marianna Hamilton. Batik on silk in white, scarlet, brown, and black.

Courtesy, artist

SIMO SOCIETY HEADDRESS.   Baga Tribe, Guinea. A hand-carved wood headpiece by a primitive tribesman has several motifs that can be used for batik designs. For instance, the overall shape with its repeat curves can be drawn, distorted, and stylized. The shapes in the ear can suggest a repeat design. The circles and chevrons within the head can be used for border and interior designs. Observe how Jennifer Lew employed similar lines and circles in her geometrical batiks on pages 74, 75.

Courtesy, The Art Institute of Chicago

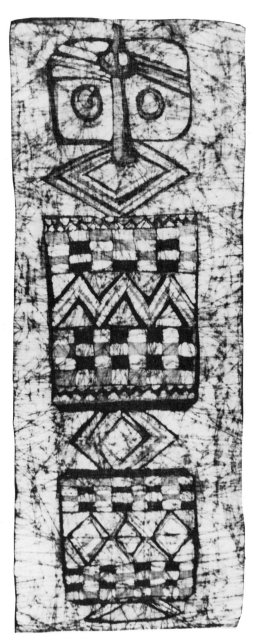

EASTER ISLAND IMAGE. Dona Meilach. White, beige, brown, and black on muslin. 46 inches high, 19 inches wide.

PRIMITIVE TOYS *(detail)*. Iswarini and Soemi-hardjo. Batik on silk. Fantastic figures from a past world or a dream world can be developed.
Courtesy, First Editions, San Jose, Calif.

AFRICAN SCULPTURE. Dolores Ashley-Harris. Wall hanging on cotton velveteen in white, blue, green, red, and black. When primary colors are used on the same composition, it is usually necessary to boil off or iron out the waxes between dyes and to rewax to keep the primary colors pure. Otherwise, the combinations of primary colors will mix. Primary colors also can be applied directly rather than by dipping.

DESIGNS FROM NATURE

Designs from nature are particularly abundant if you open your eyes and begin to think about the shapes you see. The beauty of natural shapes is that many of them also can be interpreted as geometrical designs. For decorating textiles, combining images that nature offers with circles, rectangles, and so on, opens up an entire approach for the person who thinks he can't design a thing.

As an exercise, cut an apple in half and observe the shapes; really look at them. What is the shape of the core in relation to the whole apple? What is the shape of a seed in relation to the core and the apple? Sketch these

This photo of jellyfish pulsating in a pond was taken because it suggested a possibility for a batik design. The groupings and overlapping of circles with patterns within was then interpreted in the batik (right) by Bill Hinz. Six different artists could interpret it six different ways.

shapes on paper, as an exercise, and then begin to change them slightly so they do not resemble the original apple; now they are simply shapes that can be related to one another in a design. You could make one entire composition of only one apple; or you could superimpose several parts of the shape on one or more circles for a design. The trick is to use something from nature as a beginning and then proceed to create different applications. Designs from nature are as close as your refrigerator, your garden, the park, the beach, and the forest preserve.

JELLYFISH.   Bill Hinz. Direct dye application on white velveteen. 38 inches high, 38 inches wide.

Collection, Dr. & Mrs. Mel Meilach

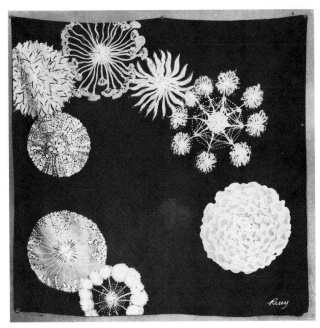

SNOWFLAKES.   Ruey Morelli. 36-inch silk scarf.
Placement is off center with three of the shapes
purposely cut off at the edges.

SCARF.   Ruey Morelli. Geometric designs are
combined with leaf shapes and run diagonally
across the silk square.

All photos, courtesy artist

LEAVES.   Ruey Morelli. Silk hanging.
This very orderly arrangement of
leaves is highly stylized and the designs freely interpreted by the artist.

SUMMER. Judith Irany. Batik on silk. Flowers that have a playful appearance are another example of how nature's objects can be applied to original batik designs.

LANDSCAPE. Marian L. Martin. Blue-gray batik background with foreground trees painted on directly with acrylics.
Photo, James R. Pelton

YELLOW RIVER. Bets Ramsey. China silk. 22 inches high, 16 inches wide. White with yellows and greens.

CHRYSALIS. Bernice Colman. Batik on silk wall hanging. Predominantly pinks and lavenders on white. 80 inches high, 44 inches wide. Shapes are based on a cutaway microscopic view of the pupa of a butterfly.

Courtesy, artist

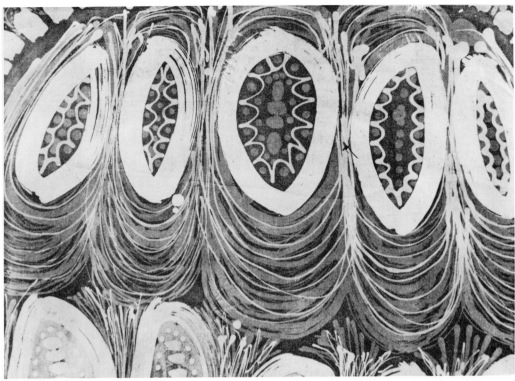

CHRYSALIS (details—top and bottom). Bernice Colman. Almost any portion of these shapes can suggest sections or entire compositions for batik designs.

Courtesy, artist

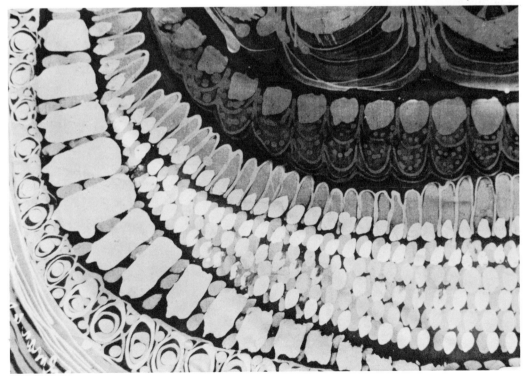

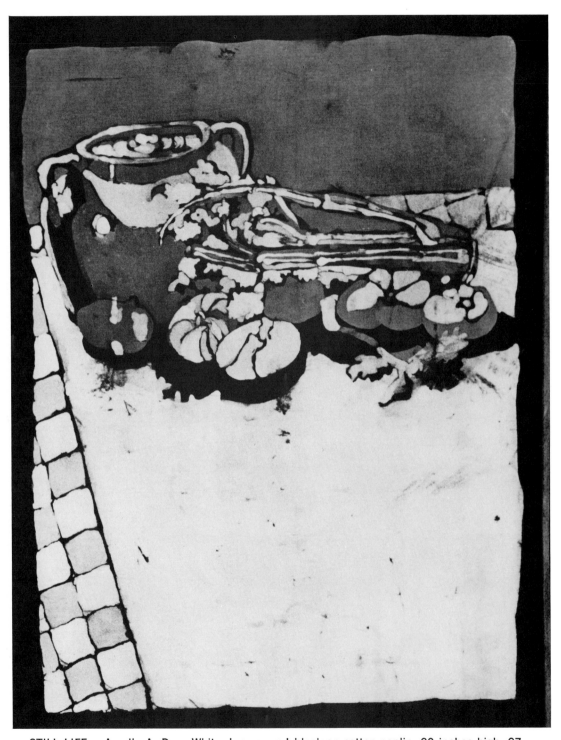

STILL LIFE. Arnelle A. Dow. White, brown, and black on cotton poplin. 20 inches high, 27 inches wide. A very painterly approach is also readily adaptable to textile design.

Courtesy, artist

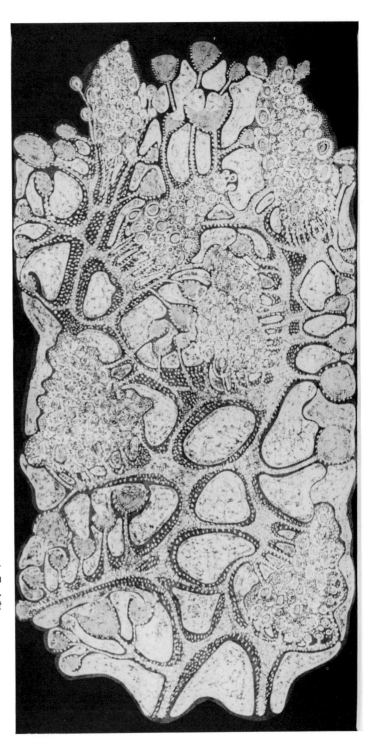

LILAC BUSH. Marie Salwon-
chik. Shades of yellow and brown
on silk. 6 feet high, 3 feet wide.
Courtesy, artist

RED YARDAGE. Mari Eagerton. A design placed along only one side of the fabric can be very successful.

Courtesy, artist

FLORAL. Lucille Bealmer. White, pink, and magenta on cotton nainsook. 8 feet high, 3 feet wide. Splashy, abstract floral design was freely drawn in wax without presketching.

Photo, Steve Terivilliger

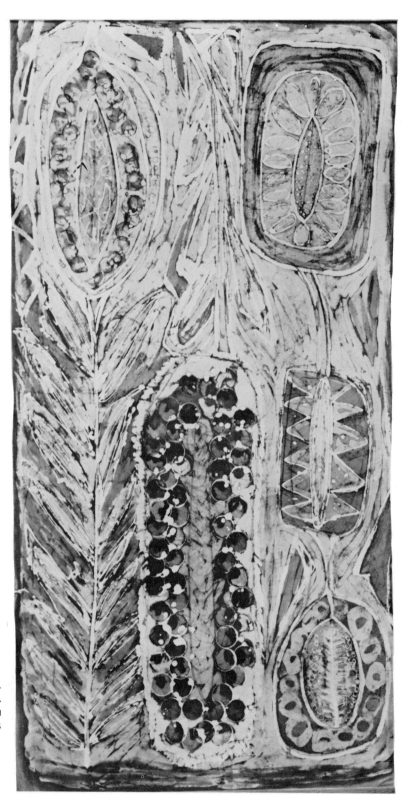

POMEGRANATES.
Blanche Carstenson.
Direct dye application
on muslin. 72 inches
high, 36 inches wide.

HORSE. Judith Irany. Batik on silk. The gesture of the horse has been quickly captured to give the feeling of both realism and simplified abstraction. The animal is centered in the space offered by the fabric.

DRAGON. Ruey Morelli. The fantastic colors suggested by the mythical animal can be beautifully created in brilliant and overdyed colors unique to batik. The animal is off-centered, which gives a feeling of unrest. Texture is suggested.

Courtesy, artist

CATS A PLENTY. Viggo Holm Madsen. Pinks, pale oranges, reds, browns, and blacks on cotton. 40 inches high, 30 inches wide. A primitive loose design depicts the artist's four cats. Lines have been created with the tjanting.
Collection, Dr. & Mrs. J. Sherman, New York
Photo, Thomas Eddy

KNIGHT. Susan Lobe. Cotton. 40 inches high, 30 inches wide. Another interpretation of an imaginary scene with a horse.

Courtesy, artist

DESIGNS FROM SYMBOLISM AND POETRY

"IN THE MIDST OF THE PLAIN SINGS THE SKYLARK FREE OF ALL THINGS." Carolyn Patterson. One of three panels on silk inspired by Haiku poetry. Each panel is 6 feet high, 3 feet wide. Colors used are white, yellow, green, and black.

Courtesy, artist

IN THE ROOM . . . Joyce Stack. Batik on linen. 15 inches by 15 inches. Imagery inspired by lines in the poem "The Love Song of J. Alfred Prufrock," by T. S. Eliot.

Collection, Mr & Mrs. Eric Peterson
Saugatuck, Mich.

SUPERSTAR (detail). Carolyn Patterson. Shades of gold, wine, and brown on linen. 44 inches high, 33 inches wide. Repeat images in different color relationships suggested by the rock opera Jesus Christ Superstar.

Photo, Greg Brown

SAMBURU. Robin Anderson. Batik on calico. 60 inches high, 30 inches wide. Images based on tribal people of Kenya.

Courtesy, The Vorpal Gallery, San Francisco

SELF PORTRAIT WITH BLACK LAKE.   Stephen Blumrich. Batik on cotton. 25 inches high,
38 inches wide. Mr. Blumrich successfully overdyes rich colors and may use from twelve to
twenty-four dippings for a single piece.

BAD DREAM.   Stephen Blumrich. Batik on cotton. 25 inches high, 46 inches wide.

AND THE NIGHT SHALL BE FILLED WITH MUSIC.   Mildred Breen. Batik on cotton.
Courtesy, Kretschmer Gallery, New York

PEOPLE AS SUBJECTS

MALE AND FEMALE—
Eleanor Levine. Linen. 15
inches high, 12 inches
wide. Predominantly
oranges and reds.

SALOME. Susan Lobe.
Cotton. 36 inches high, 30
inches wide. Gold, orange,
reds brushed on. Some
blues over reds to get purples. Blue over yellow areas
to get green. Some black.
Final crackle in dark blue
leaving skin areas only
lightly crackled.

Courtesy, artist

MASAI MAIDENS.   Robin Anderson. Batik panel shows a very controlled, carefully articulated form against a freely designed background.

Courtesy, The Vorpal Gallery, San Francisco

6

APPLYING DYES DIRECTLY

BATIK techniques, so far, have dealt with immersing the fabric in a dyebath. Another popular practice is to apply coloring directly to the fabric to achieve effects you can't get by dipping. Direct dye application may be used for entire compositions or in conjunction with immersing. It can be used to make lines and colors bolder on a previously batiked fabric. The reverse may be accomplished also; a design can be applied directly to the fabric, then waxed over, and portions batiked. Direct dyeing application may be successfully combined with silk screen, block printing, and airbrush spraying. Infinite possibilities present themselves for creating more striking compositions if you know how to use both techniques. You should also become familiar with types of pigment colors as well as dyes.

Dyes may be applied directly with or without resist materials. Waxes may be used and sometimes the resist can be a piece of paper placed on the fabric to leave a white space when dye is sprayed on with a spray nozzle. Starch and flour combinations and vegetable shortenings will resist color when the fabric is not dipped in a solution that will wash them away during soaking; special cold resist materials are available also. It isn't necessary to coat the fabric front and back with the resist when you apply dyes directly.

The working surface will depend on how you approach the technique and any method is acceptable so long as it does the job. You can work with the fabric stretched on a frame. Often it is more efficient to pin the fabric flat on a padded work surface. Padding may be a sheet of foam rubber about ⅜ inch thick, an old blanket, a piece of carpet felt, or newspapers placed on a hard, level table. Cover this with a sheet of muslin and either clamp, tape, or pin all materials to the tabletop to prevent them from sliding. Then stretch the fabric to be decorated over the muslin and adhere it to the surface with T pins. It is easier to work on a piece of fabric that is smaller than your work surface so you won't have to move it around. Use a T square for aligning edges and lines in patterns.

◄

UNTITLED *(detail).*   Bill Hinz. Fiber reactive dyes applied directly to cotton velveteen display color blends and linear effects that are not possible with the dip-dyeing method.

DYEING AND FIXING

The dyeing and fixing procedures for direct application differ slightly from those used in dipping. The reason is that the fixation of dyes into the fibers requires moisture with an "assistant" over a period of time. This occurs in the immersing process. In direct application the long moisture procedure in the presence of salt is absent. This is compensated for by using a chemical solution with the dyestuff.

Often a thickened dye solution is desirable to give body to the mixture so it can be controlled more readily. A thickening agent should be soluble in water and chemically inert so it will not react with the dye and be easily removed from the material during the wash off.

The most popular dyes for direct application are the fiber reactive class under the trade name Procion M, distributed by Fibrec, Hi Dye, Dylon (see pages 256–259). They have brilliant colors and are highly colorfast. In addition they react with different fabrics in strange and wonderful ways as they creep into the fibers and spread. Often a mixture of colors will separate soon after it hits the fabric and the tones of color achieved are striking.

For direct dye application, fabrics must be washed to remove sizing. Most satisfactory fabrics are mercerized cotton, Indian Head cotton, viscose rayon, velveteen, corduroy, linen, terrycloth, and silk.

For direct dyeing, fiber reactive dyes are added to a mixture of Calgon, urea, and water for a thin solution. For a thicker solution, sodium alginate is added to the chemical water and then the dye powder added to that. Just before using, baking soda and washing soda must be added; these cause the dyes to react and to couple with the fibers. Formulas for using thickeners are given on page 112. Several distributors are marketing a mixture of these hard-

Lines, shapes, and color repairs can be made with any of a variety of pigment colors, including waterproof inks, waterproof felt-tip pens, textile paints, dye crayons, acrylic paints, and others available from art-craft suppliers. They may be applied from the tubes, from squeeze bottles, with brushes, sponges, or whatever will give the effect you want.

to-locate thickening chemicals and offering various ways to use them. In addition, when dyes are applied directly to the fabrics, the colors may be set by using heat and moisture such as steaming, steam ironing, or baking as described on pages 113–115.

PIGMENTS

Coloring for fabrics in the form of *pigments* is also popular for direct application. Pigments coat a fiber rather than becoming part of it as do dyes, and they are usually more opaque than dyes. Many are very permanent. Textile paints, already thickened, are extremely versatile. They also may be thinned down with water so they can be sprayed, dribbled, or thinly brushed on for specific effects. Fixing with heat is required and manufacturer's instructions for specific products should be followed.

Many kinds of coloring agents that will adhere to fabrics have been used by artists including acrylic paints, waterproof felt-tip pens, India inks, watercolor concentrates, silk screen paints, and others that you will find in craft catalogs and shops. Always experiment before applying them to a good design.

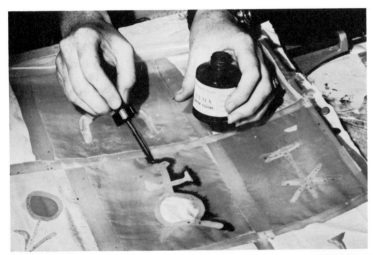

The working surface may be the fabric tacked to a frame. Here the resist is wax and permanent watercolors are being applied to the open area with the eyedropper applicator that comes with the product. The dry watercolor line can be waxed, then the entire fabric dipped in dye.

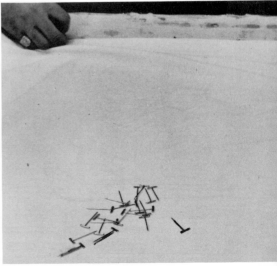

For overall direct dye application the best work surface is a hard tabletop padded with foam rubber or felt and a sheet of muslin. The work fabric is carefully stretched and pinned to the table's surface keeping the warp and weft of the fabric as straight as possible to prevent distortion of the pattern when it is unpinned.

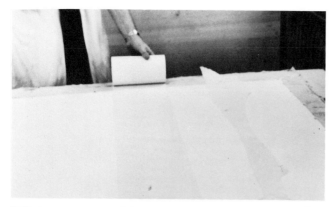

In the following series, Bill Hinz demonstrates the use of fiber reactive dyes on white cotton velveteen. He uses paper toweling to block out, or "resist," color. The toweling is rolled across the tacked down fabric and torn into shapes.

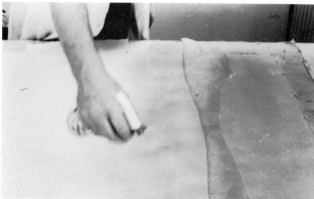

A thin mixture of dye with chemical water is applied with a spray bottle and the colors begin to bleed into the fabric as they spread.

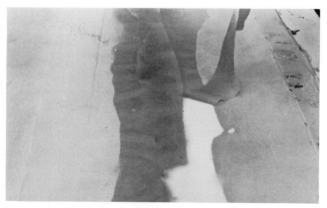

Mr. Hinz lifts the paper to show how it held back the dye so the white area was retained.

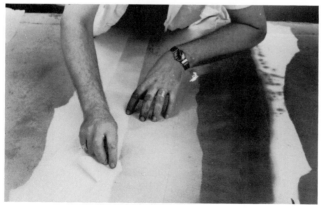

Additional layers of paper toweling are placed across the first colors and torn into new shapes.

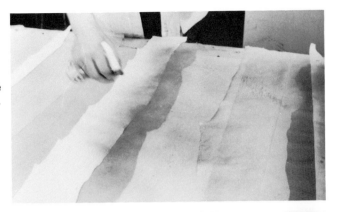

More colors and darker shades will be applied as the colors and shapes build up.

Holding the spray nozzle low and sideways and adjusting to a stream setting for larger splotches of color yields a different texture from those achieved with an overall even spray.

Colors begin to bleed on the fabric. If two or more colors have been premixed they separate with exciting results. For instance a green shade may separate and yield areas of blue and yellow around it. Later, a black line can be added for emphasis.

When the spray adjustment is set for the heaviest spray, still another series of shapes can be achieved.

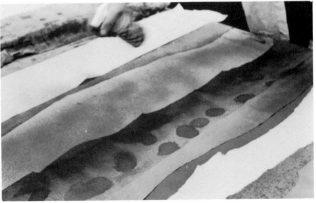

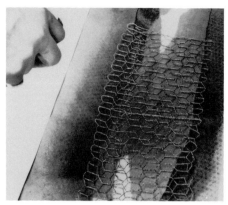

Other possible ways to build up design can be used. Spray over a folded piece of chicken wire.

Thicken the dye slightly and use it with a squeeze bottle from catsup or hair tint. Draw with it, make dots with it.

Assemble a group of found objects and spray over them with the spray thin or heavy.

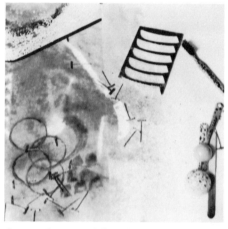

Spoon shapes, sticks, plastic shapes, anything can be used as a "resist" much as a stencil is used to achieve design.

Dipping a sponge in slightly thickened dye and then applying it to the fabric results in another texture.

The dye spreads and the colors separate and overlap. Fiber reactive dyes are unique in this quality.

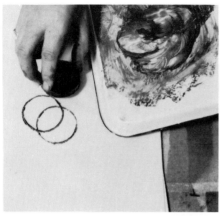

Designs can be printed with edges of objects such as the top of a spray can.

A brushstroke

Dabs from the end of the brush

A large sweeping brushstroke

Toothbrush spatters

A hand print

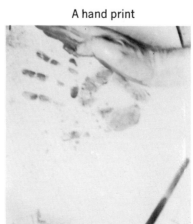

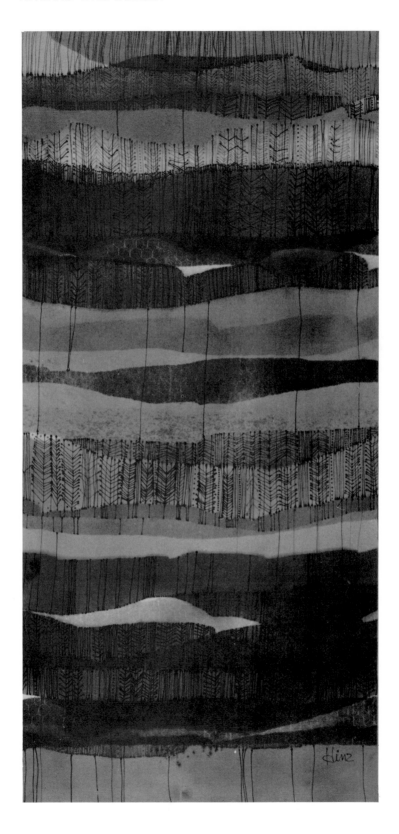

UNTITLED. Bill Hinz. Fiber reactive dyes applied directly to white cotton velveteen. 24 inches square. Fabric is brought around back of plain wood frame and stapled.

UNTITLED. Bill Hinz. Orange and black fiber reactive dyes on white velveteen. 30 inches high, 16 inches wide.

◄

UNTITLED. Bill Hinz. The finished piece illustrated in steps 1 through 8. 6 feet high, 4 feet wide. Fiber reactive dyes applied directly to white velveteen. Says Mr. Hinz, "Velveteen is particularly adaptable to direct application because the nap gives the colors another dimension. The dyes should be allowed to dry thoroughly which helps set the colors. The fabric should be steamed, rinsed in cool and hot water, then washed according to directions."

MIXING FIBER REACTIVE DYES FOR DIRECT APPLICATION

For a thin dye solution that can be sprayed, the dyestuff is added to a mixture of chemical water. For a thick solution, sodium alginate is mixed with the chemical water and then the dyestuff is added.

Chemical water stock solution. Yield: 1 quart, which may be stored indefinitely.
1 teaspoon Calgon (from the grocery store)
10 tablespoons urea (from a chemical supply house)
2 cups hot water
2 cups cold water

Use a quart jar and stir the Calgon and urea into 2 cups of hot water. When dissolved add the cold water and shake well.

TO USE FOR THIN APPLICATIONS, for spraying, brushing, sprinkling.

To 1 quart of chemical water add:
1 teaspoon dye for pale value
4 teaspoons dye for medium value
8 or more teaspoons for dark value

With the dye added the shelf life is about 28 days at which time the colors will lighten.

4 teaspoons baking soda
1 teaspoon washing soda dissolved in a small amount of hot water

Procedure: just before using, measure the required amount of dye powder into a small container and paste with a small amount of chemical water to dissolve thoroughly. Then add dye to total amount of chemical water. Add the required amount of *baking and washing soda just before using.* Soda is the last addition and must not be forgotten: it causes the dye to start reacting.

FOR THICK APPLICATION

Sodium alginate is added to the clear chemical water stock solution. Sprinkle 1 to 4 teaspoons of sodium alginate over 1 quart of chemical water. Stir constantly or shake vigorously for about 10 minutes or stir in an electric mixer or blender. It can be used immediately or allowed to set overnight and become smoother. The thickened stock solution should be stored in a covered bottle and in a cool place.

TO USE: A full quart of thickener is rarely used for one color. So determine the amount of dye you need for the value you are using and dissolve in a small amount of thickener; then add to it as much thickener as you think you will need for the specific application. Usually you will use ½ to 1 cup. Dissolve the proportionate amount of baking soda and washing soda in a small amount of plain water and add. (For 1 cup of thickener use 1 teaspoon baking soda and ¼ teaspoon washing soda in only enough water to dissolve it.)

Thickened applications may be used for squeeze bottles, brushing on, and printing. The method of application and the fabric determine the

WRAPPING THE FABRIC
FOR STEAMING

Dyed fabrics must be carefully wrapped in newspapers, paper toweling, or thin cloth for steaming so none of the fabric touches itself and it is smooth between the layers. If wax has been used, iron out as much as possible and wash fabric in either benzine, white gas or cleaning fluid. Spread paper toweling under and over the fabric.

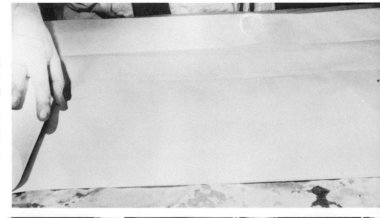

Fold the fabric and both layers of paper over carefully so the fabric does not touch itself.

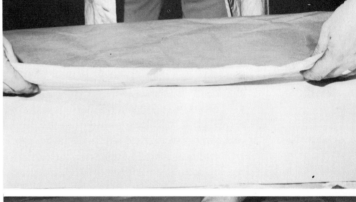

Roll or fold the fabric and paper...

...into a loose bundle and tie it so that you can undo it rapidly. Tie bundle so it will fit into the steaming vessel you will use and *does not touch the sides or top of the pot.*

viscosity. Thickener can be thinned by adding a little more chemical water. It is usually wise to mix the solution thicker and then thin it down as required. Always experiment. For brushing use a coarse nylon bristle brush; natural bristle brushes will soften and become uncontrollable.

Note: Turquoise and black, when used with the thickener, behave similarly to other colors except that washing soda should be substituted for all or part of the baking soda. Black is difficult to work with and may need to be fixed longer.

OTHER FORMULA: **Fibrec packages a premixed combination of urea, Calgon, and sodium alginate. The thickener is blended with water in an electric mixer and allowed to stand for 15 to 20 minutes. The dye powder is added to the thickener.** *For a cold process the fabric is first washed in washing soda* **but not rinsed. The dye, added to the thickener, is applied to the dry fabric and allowed to dry. No heat fixing is required. Finish with cold and hot water rinses, then a final wash in hot soapy water.** *For a hot process:* **add 1 teaspoon of baking soda per cup of thickener just prior to adding the dye. Follow finishing procedure above.**

STEAMING AND OTHER FIXING METHODS

Many setups can be improvised for fixing the dried print. For steaming, a pot must be deep enough to accommodate the wrapped fabric without its touching the top or sides. A large preserving kettle set on the kitchen stove will hold a 3-yard length of medium weight fabric. Heavy fabrics should be rolled in one direction and steamed; then unrolled, rerolled in the opposite direction, and steamed again. Sheer fabric need not be rerolled. The water should be steaming before the fabric is put in the pot. When there is a strong smell of urea, the fabric is usually steamed sufficiently.

TO SET UP THE STEAMER

1. Set a platform in the bottom of the pan. It should allow for 2 inches of water and be about 4 inches above the water level. The platform can be a wire bottle rack or a coffee can with top and bottom cut out. Place a plate or wire cake rack over that for a platform.
2. The coiled, tied fabric must be protected from spattering or from drops of condensation by placing it between layers of padding and newspapers. Use a layer of felt, padded cloth, paper towels, or newspapers on top of the platform, then put the coiled fabric on that. Cover the coil with another layer of padded materials. Materials should be a slightly larger diameter than the coiled fabric but they must not touch the sides or top of the pot.
3. Place a thick pad of newspapers or cloth (old mattress pads are good) over the opening of the pot and extending out from it.
4. Put the cover on the pot and weight it if necessary with bricks or a piece of wood. This causes the pressure to build up while still allowing enough steam to escape for safety. Bring water to boil, lift cover, and place fabric on platform with paper and pad on top of it and replace cover. Steam for 5 to 30 minutes depending upon weight and nature of the fabric. You will have to experiment. When steaming is done, open pot carefully and unwrap fabric as quickly as possible.

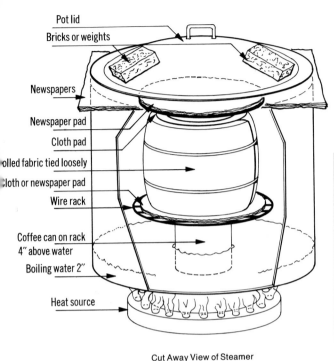

Pot lid
Bricks or weights
Newspapers
Newspaper pad
Cloth pad
olled fabric tied loosely
cloth or newspaper pad
Wire rack
Coffee can on rack
4″ above water
Boiling water 2″
Heat source

Cut Away View of Steamer

Bill Hinz uses an enamel canning vessel across two burners of a hot plate for steaming at the School of the Art Institute of Chicago.

FINISHING

Rinse the fabric in deep cold water baths until the water is clear. Work fast so excess dye or print paste does not stain other parts of the cloth. Continue rinsing in baths of increasing warmth until no more dye comes out. Place fabric in hot water with ½ ounce of liquid soap for each 2 gallons of water. Do final wash in a washing machine.

MORE FIXING METHODS

Any one of these other fixing methods can be used:

1. **Dry-bake coiled fabric in an oven for 5 minutes at 285°.**
2. **Steam-bake fabric.** Loosely fold fabric between paper toweling and wrap. Place on oven shelf. Place pan of water large enough to cover shelf on rack below fabric. Bake at 285° for 15 to 30 minutes depending on size of fabric. For a large piece refold in opposite direction and rebake.
3. **Air-dry in warm humid atmosphere for 1 to 2 days.**
4. **Place the wrapped, coiled fabric on papers between cloth and place in a sauna for 15 to 30 minutes and set at 250°.**
5. **Iron for 5 minutes with the iron set at 285° or at steam or warm.**
6. **Use a commercial steam cabinet. Use an autoclave from a hospital.**

Under proper steaming conditions, the dye will enter the fabric and set. If the steam is too moist, the colors may run. If it is too dry or if the dye solution contained too much thickener and the dye is not absorbed properly, it may wash away in the finishing process.

REMINISCING. Leo F. Twiggs. 32 inches high, 28 inches wide. Batik with some direct application of color.

Collection, Mr. & Mrs. Francis T. Draine, Columbus, S.C.

Mr. Twiggs at work on *Reminiscing.*

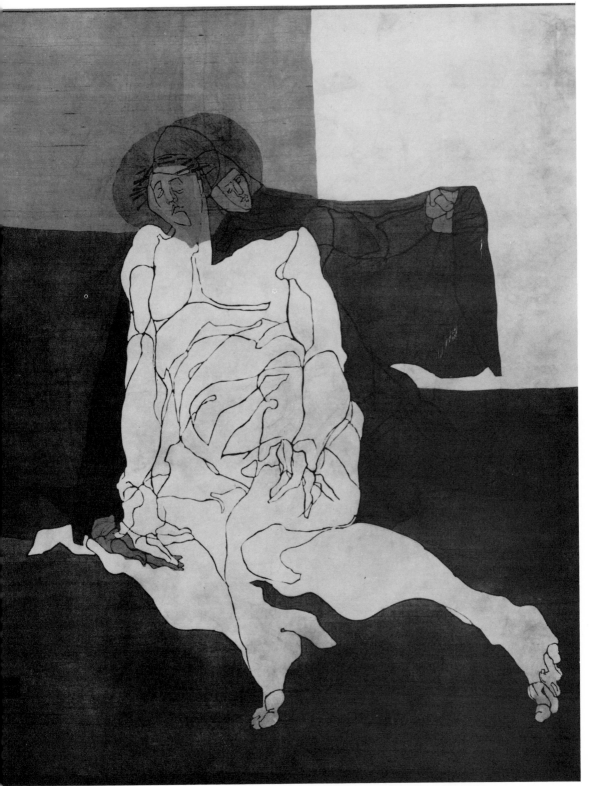

PIETA. Joseph Almyda. Batik on silk wall hanging. 50 inches high, 40 inches wide.
Courtesy, American Crafts Council

COLD RESISTS AND TEXTILE PAINTS

Dorland's textile wax is a cold wax easily used for resisting water-soluble, permanent-color Versatex . . . a pigment for painting directly on fabric. Dorland's has a pastelike consistency that can be used directly from the jar. It can also be thinned with 10 parts water to 1 part wax for use in a plastic squeeze bottle. After coloring, the wax can be scraped or rinsed off in warm water.

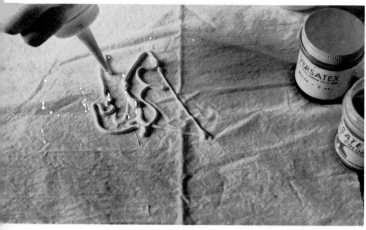

Applying thinned wax from a squeeze bottle. Allow to dry before painting . . . several hours or overnight. For batik, it must dry hard and then it will crackle.

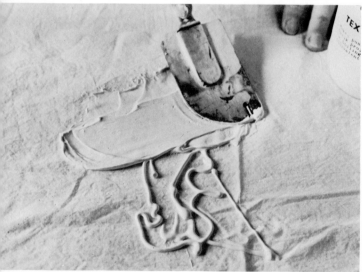

It can be applied with a spatula, a spoon, or your fingers using the consistency directly from the bottle. One advantage is that if you change your mind about its placement, wipe it off with a towel while it is still damp. If it is dry, pick it off or lift with a palette knife.

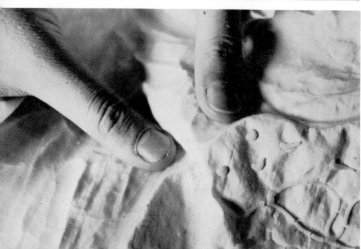

To crackle, break the wax by gently folding the fabric. Do not use this wax for dipping because it does not penetrate the fabric and it is water soluble. Do not use with fiber reactive dyes as they will creep under the wax.

Apply Versatex, a textile pigment paint, over the dry wax with a brush, sponge, roller or palette knife. Versatex can be used as it comes from the jar or thinned with water. For squeeze bottle application use 1 part color to 5 parts water. Allow to dry.

Remove Dorland's Wax by dipping the fabric in very hot water about 3 times. This also sets the pigment color. Reapply wax to hold color where desired for additional color buildup and repeat waxing and painting steps. When all the wax is out, iron the colored fabric from the back to set the color permanently. For transparency and pastel colors, use special Versatex Extender. Avoid letting wax go down drains. Use a catch screen in drain and when wax is out of fabric turn on cold water to reharden waste wax, then empty from sink.

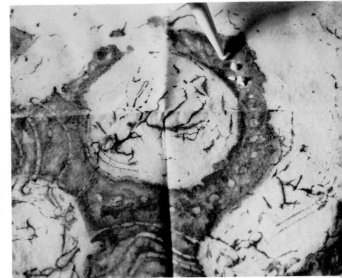

Areas of color can be added for accent.

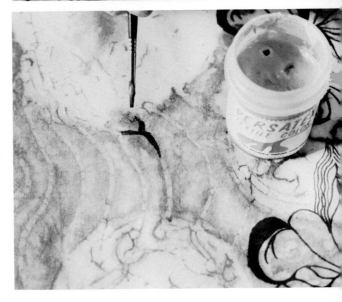

A silk screen can be effectively used with batik. The designed screen is placed over the fabric, and Versatex is squeezed across the screen.

The design is transferred to the fabric over the batiked crackled design. This shows the kind of line and crackle obtained by this method.

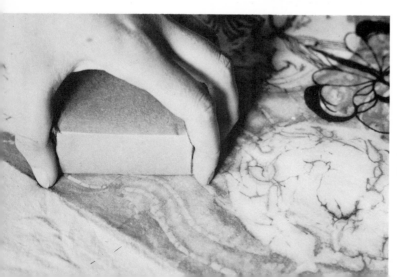

The block printing technique may also be used effectively.

MOUNTAINSIDE *(detail)*. Jan Wagstaff. Direct application with block printing and silk screen over a background of batik using cold textile wax.

FABRIC YARDAGE. Sister Mary Remy Revor. Batik and block print.

Courtesy, artist

OTHER RESISTS FOR DIRECT APPLICATION

Often you will want to resist a small area quickly. The easiest method is to use a vegetable shortening such as Crisco or Mazola oil on the area. Place the dye, pigment, or bleach around the resist and it will hold the color. Apply shortenings with a brush, fingers, spoon, knife, or spatula. A serrated-blade knife gives an interesting texture.

A flour-paste resist material can be mixed using 3 tablespoons of flour and 1 cup of water cooked in the top of a double boiler until it has an almost transparent appearance. Stir while cooking and, when thick, brush or spoon it onto the fabric while hot. Brush on dyes or pigments. Do not immerse as the dipping will wash out the resist. Remove the resist by washing after the coloring has dried.

A starch-paste resist can be mixed with 1 tablespoon white flour, 1 table-spoon rice flour, ½ tablespoon powdered laundry starch, and 1¼ cups hot water. Mix the dry ingredients in a little cold water and remove all lumps. Add hot water and cook in top of double boiler for about 15 minutes. Use while hot.

Other paste resists can be made from combinations of rice powder, bran powder, salt, and slaked lime and water. Such formulas are for the person who wants to experiment with specific methods used by various cultures. Formulas are available with the ingredients from suppliers of Japanese art materials (Aiko).

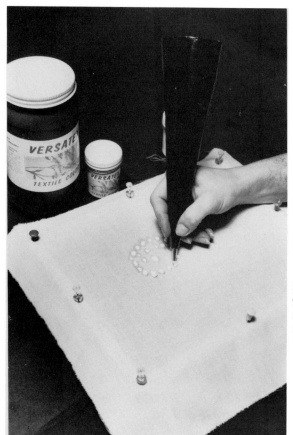

Flour and other paste resists can be applied from cardboard tubes fitted with different size brass endings. They are used in the same way as a cookie decorator.

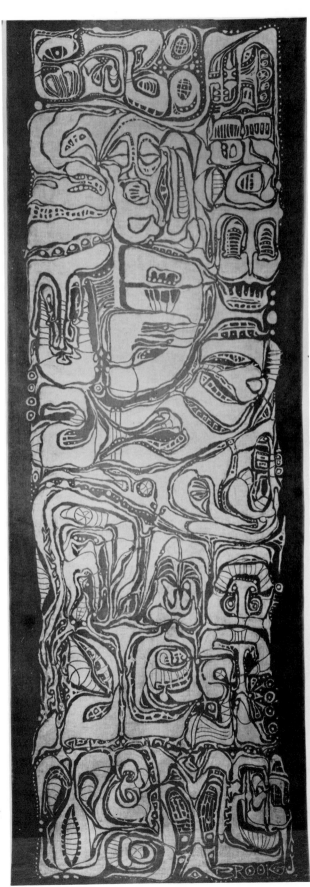

GET OFF STANDARD TIME. Lois
Brooks. Starch-paste resist used
with natural indigo dye on cotton
broadcloth following a traditional
process called "Adire Eleko" used
by the Yoruba peoples of Nigeria.
*Collection, Mr. & Mrs. Robert
Hinerfeld, Brentwood, Calif.*

The album, above, with the pages from it that follow, are by Benita Cullinan. They illustrate the high degree of detail and even hard edge that can be achieved by direct dye application. All are on cotton velveteen and combined with stitchery.

Each page represents someone in the artist's family; hence the "family album" theme, with personal symbolism. This page shows her young brother and his dog with a duck . . . see detail opposite.

The whole family together. Details show the use of stitchery with colored yarns.

Detail of photo *(left)* with stitchery.

QUILT. Benita Cullinan. Patchwork, direct dye quilt in cotton velveteen edged and lined with silk. Padding is of Dacron.

COUCH. Benita Cullinan. Framed direct dye with padded cushions that extend out as soft sculpture. 10 inches high, 12 inches wide. Some stitchery.

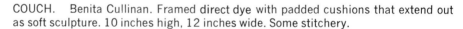

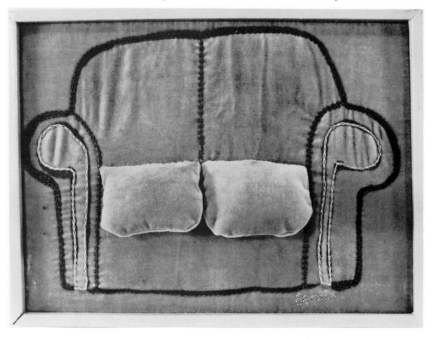

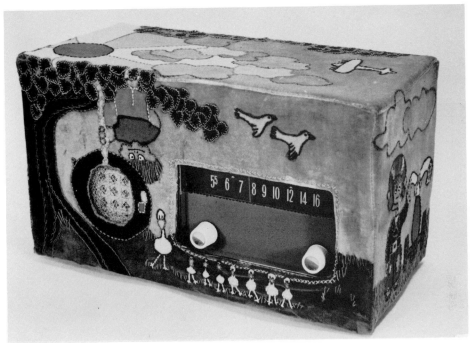

RADIO COVER. Benita Cullinan.

CLOCK FACE. Benita Cullinan.

128

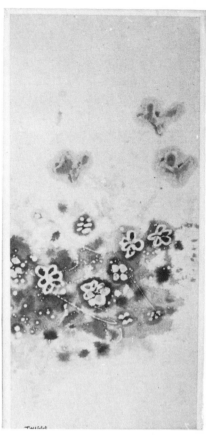

THIS SPRING. Leo F. Twiggs. Combination of immersion and direct dye applications. Two panels, each 34 inches high, 17 inches wide.

Courtesy, artist

REVOLVING DOOR. Linda Menger. 29 inches high, 19 inches wide. Direct dye application using an airbrush on fabric.

Courtesy, artist

WELCOME TO THE AMUSU.　Linda Menger. Dye applied directly to fabric with an airbrush. 29 inches high, 19 inches wide.

Collection, R. S. Colley, Jr.
Corpus Christi, Texas

7

PAPER BATIK

THE batik processes already discussed can be as aptly applied to paper as to fabrics. Batik on paper is easy to do in a limited space, inexpensive, and fun. You can get a variety of results. It is excellent for classroom use at every age level. Its application as an artistic medium is being more fully explored as its versatility is being recognized.

Paper batik can be accomplished both by immersing and by direct dye application. The type of paper used and the finished result desired will determine the best technique. For immersing, watercolor, drawing, or heavy Oriental papers are most satisfactory because they will not disintegrate from repeated dippings into dye solution.

For direct application Oriental papers are especially nice because they are interwoven with fibers that give them strength and texture and may be easily crackled. They are available in a variety of textures and colors. Often only a single color application yields a beautiful two color composition. Poster board, chipboard, and similar heavy paper can be used, too, but you cannot get the crackle.

All dyes seem to have an affinity to paper. The cold water fiber reactive dyes are particularly easy to use with brilliant color results. You don't have to worry about washfastness as with fabrics. Paper should not be placed in sunlight. Often shade and artificial lighting will fade them somewhat. Pigment colors such as watercolors and textile paints are effective but they are not as transparent as the dyes. Moistening the paper before dyeing aids in the dispersion of the dyes for additional soft effects.

Use the same wax resists as those described for fabric batik. In addition,

◄

COMPOSITION #53. Joyce Wexler. White, beige, and brown on wood-chip-textured Oriental mulberry paper. 25 inches high, 18 inches wide. The piece is mounted on cardboard, placed under a mat board, and framed without glass.

The setup for paper batik is the same as that used for textile batik. Small batches of color used for direct application are mixed in disposable paper cups. Cotton tips are handy for stirring and applying color. Cutout paper shapes are used for collage on batik.

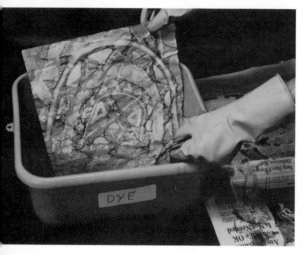

Papers can be dyed by immersing but do not let them soak in the dye solution; just dip them and dry immediately by placing them on or between paper to blot off excess moisture. Let batik dry thoroughly after each dye coat before rewaxing. Very thin papers are not successful for immersing as they tend to disintegrate. Use heavy papers such as watercolor, bond, and drawing papers.

rubber cement may be applied to the paper. After the dye color has dried, the rubber cement is rolled off. Use a sturdy paper that will withstand rubbing. Bleaches may be used very carefully for discharge dyeing. Always experiment with a specific paper and bleach solution to be sure the bleach will not eat up the paper.

You really don't need a frame for paper batiks; work them directly over a sheet of plastic or wax paper. If the waxes cause the paper to stick to the work surface, heat a brush with wax and place it between the two layers until the wax is melted sufficiently for separation.

Holes are an inevitable hazard of paper batik. Prepare an extra strip of paper for use for possible patching. Patches usually blend in better if the edges are torn, not cut, and then glued or waxed and ironed onto the front or back of the paper. If the batik is torn beyond repair use parts of it as collage on future compositions.

Batik with collage has been beautifully developed by artist Joyce Wexler who demonstrates her methods beginning on page 134. Collage papers used included magazine cutouts, scrolls, singed paper, photographs, fold- and tie-dyed papers, and calligraphy. Mrs. Wexler uses fiber reactive dyes but omits the washing soda fix as it tends to dry and leave residue on the paper after a few weeks. Often, she eliminates salt, also. Dyes are brushed on in a thin solution, no thickening agents used. The heat generated during the ironing process sets the colors.

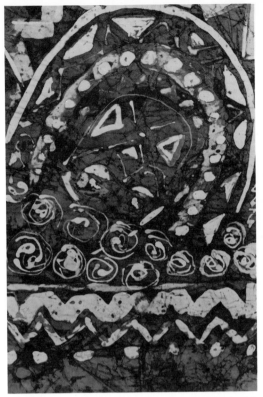

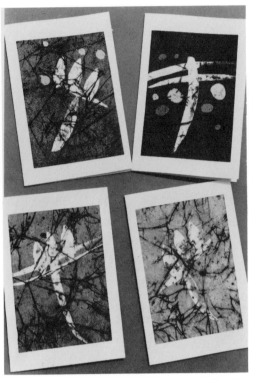

UNTITLED. Dona Meilach. 16 inches high, 12 inches wide. Fiber-reactive dyes on watercolor bond using yellow, pink, and black. Curls and lines made with a tjanting. Extra spotting textures result when dye is purposely left on wax so it bubbles through the wax when it is ironed.

GREETING CARDS. Diana Lawson. Small paper batiks, each 3 inches by 4 inches, are adhered to cards with dry glue. Medium weight rice paper is used for immersing. After the first wax and dye the paper is dipped in hot wax. When cool it is crackled and placed in fiber reactive dye for about 10 minutes, then removed, spread out and dried, then ironed out.

MUST SPRINGTIME FADE? Joyce Wexler. Paper batik. 17 inches high, 30 inches wide. A Haiku poem is carefully waxed, then dye applied. Observe the purposely ragged edges of the Oriental mulberry paper which is mounted on a mat board, then matted and framed.

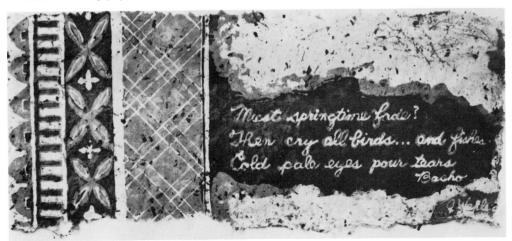

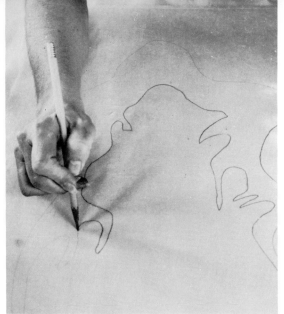

Joyce Wexler demonstrates the techniques for developing a batik with paper collage by direct dye application.

The design is traced or drawn on Oriental paper.

The collage shapes are cut out and placed within the shapes allowed for them, covering the pencil lines so they don't show after dyeing.

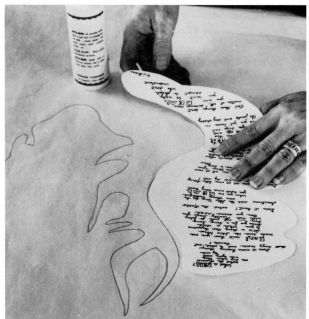

Waterproof glue is used and the paper is adhered, squeezing out the glue from under the edges. Backs of thick papers can be sanded lightly so they bond better. If the paper has a gloss finish, lightly sand the front also so it will take dye better.

After the initial papers are glued, wax the areas you wish to remain white.

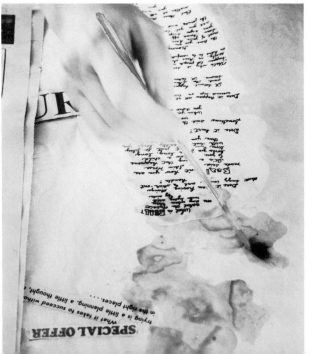

Also brush wax over some areas of the collage papers.

Brush the coat of dye over the paper and waxed portions. You can see where the dye is absorbed by the paper, but it forms splotches on the wax where it is resisted.

Use a soft rag to blot excess dye from the wax and to avoid getting the paper too wet. For a hard-edge look, use paper that will not absorb readily; for a soft blended appearance use very absorbent paper.

Use a cotton tip to apply dye to small areas or delicate portions of the paper.

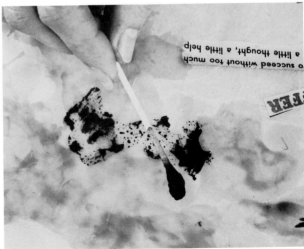

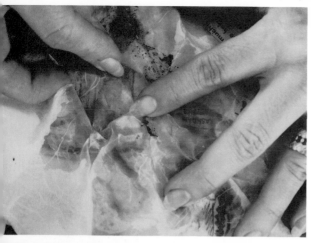

To crackle, gently bunch up the paper in the waxed areas and crease them with your fingers to break the wax.

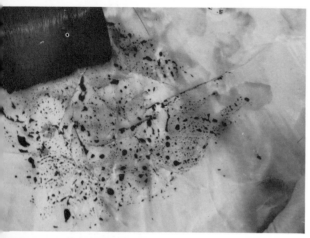

Then brush over the crackle with color; it will penetrate the cracks in the wax.

Wipe off the excess dye. If some dye remains, it will seep through the wax during ironing and yield an additional texture.

Iron the paper batik between paper layers. The first ironing can be between newspapers until almost all wax is removed; then finish with toweling to avoid transferring newsprint to the batik. If your collage papers are printed, colored illustrations, do not use too much heat over them or the printed coloring will transfer from the collage to the paper toweling and your batik will be ruined.

HOME FREE.   Joyce Wexler. Paper batik with collage on rice paper made with silk threads. 26 inches high, 23 inches wide. Collage papers are handwritten on bond paper and magazine cutouts.

OVER AND OUT.   Joyce Wexler. Paper batik. 29 inches high, 23 inches wide. Strathmore brilliant art paper.

ACHI-KOCHI. Joyce Wexler. Batik on mulberry paper. 20 inches high, 24 inches wide.

THIS CERTIFICATE ENTITLES YOU TO. Joyce Wexler. Batik on rice paper. 22 inches high, 28 inches wide.

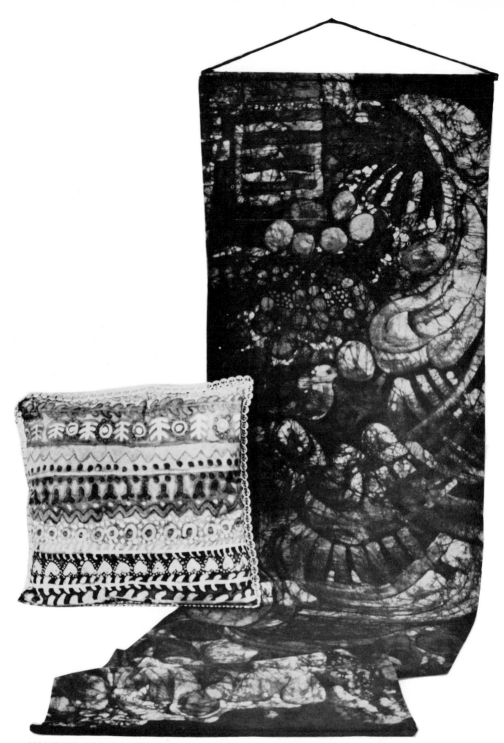

HANGING ROOM DIVIDER AND PILLOW. A long strip of well-washed old muslin sheeting was batiked to make the wall hanging using Crayola crayons as the color and wax medium. A hollow curtain rod is inserted in the hem at top; wool yarn threaded through it is used for hanging. Another curtain rod in the bottom hem anchors the hanging. The pillow is also batiked with Crayola crayons. After each strip of design was placed on the fabric, a different dye color was brushed on to vary the background hues.

Specially prepared by Binney & Smith, Inc.
Makers of Crayola crayons

8

COLORED WAX BATIK

THERE are many ways to approach batik. In the previous chapters, colorless resists were used and the color added with dyes. In this chapter, the use of colored waxes is demonstrated. The principle is simple: you combine the coloring and waxing in one application.

Colored waxes are available as crayons and colored paraffin used for candlemaking or specially prepared for batik. Each color of melted wax is "painted" directly onto fabric or paper. You can use as many colors as you like and see the color relationship develop as you work. No overdyeing and color mixing are involved. Perhaps one dyebath is desirable to fill in background and achieve crackle but it does not mix with the painted-on colors as the wax resists the dyebath. When the fabric is ironed, the wax is melted out but the wax color remains in the batik.

Colorings used in crayons and colored wax are usually not permanent so fabric batiks made by this method should be dry cleaned and not washed. It is especially adaptable to white and colored paper and if no crackle is desired the final dyebath can be eliminated or dye can be brushed on instead of dipping the paper in dye. When the colored wax buildup is too heavy, colors tend to run into each other during the ironing out. This can be minimized by setting the iron on the fabric in successive strokes to melt the wax rather than ironing back and forth. Old towels will absorb the melted wax more quickly than will newspapers when ironing.

Colored wax may be combined with immersing and direct dye applications when you want to add a primary color detail. For instance, if you want a touch of blue on yellow, brush on the blue first, then dip in yellow; the blue will not turn green.

A bonus of colored wax batik is possible. When you iron out, place a sheet of parchment or rice paper beneath the waxed batik rather than newspapers or toweling. The colors, and some of the wax from the original, will transfer to the paper beneath and result in a soft, slightly blurred duplicate composition. Sometimes, the new image can be more interesting than the original.

Colored wax batik is especially adaptable to the primary schoolroom where broken Crayola bits are usually abundant and permanency and colorfastness are not so important.

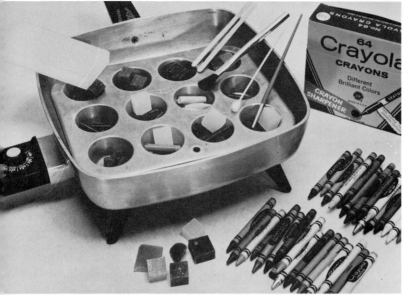

To melt colored crayons for batik, break the wax into small pieces and place in a muffin cup set in some water in an electric fry pan. Add small pieces of paraffin or beeswax to the colored wax. Melt and brush the colored wax directly onto the fabric. Keep one brush for each color and use cotton tips, sticks, spatulas, palette knives, or anything else that will transfer the color to the batik. Brushes and tools may be cleaned with carbon tetrachloride or alcohol.

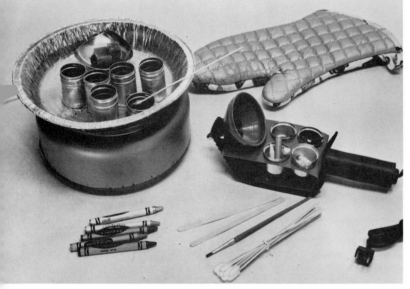

Another way to melt the wax is to use small tubes from camera film, small ashtrays, or whatever else you can improvise, placed in a pan of water on a hot plate. Watch carefully to be sure the wax does not burn. Pick up cups individually with a potholder. Wax must be hot enough to penetrate the fabric and not stay on top of it.

Applying one color next to another is the same principle as painting colors on directly. You know what colors you are getting and you can see how they relate. When working, keep the already waxed portions of your cloth away from the heat source to prevent melting. A final overall dyebath will unify the background and tie all colors together. Crush to crackle if desired.

SMALL CITY. Vivian Kline. Color from melted Crayolas mixed with paraffin was painted onto cotton allowing white spaces so that one dyebath could be used both to fill in the spaces and create the crackle throughout. Such batiks are lovely when framed in a light box with the source of light behind them.

THE SMALL CITY (above) was ironed out with a sheet of parchment beneath to absorb the wax and excess color. This is the result.

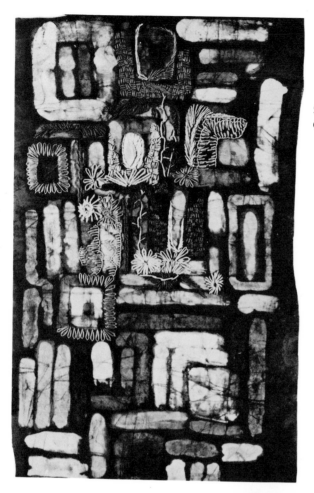

SMALL HANGING. Crayon with stitch-
ery. 18 inches high, 12 inches wide.
Prepared by Binney & Smith, Inc.
Makers of Crayola crayons

Pillow cover in process. Each flower section has been painted with a different
color melted *Crayola* mixed with paraffin.
After waxing, a dye was brushed over the
flowers to fill in the background in a
contrasting color. Stitchery added.
Prepared by Binney & Smith, Inc.
Makers of Crayola crayons

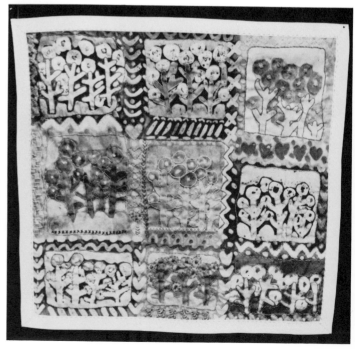

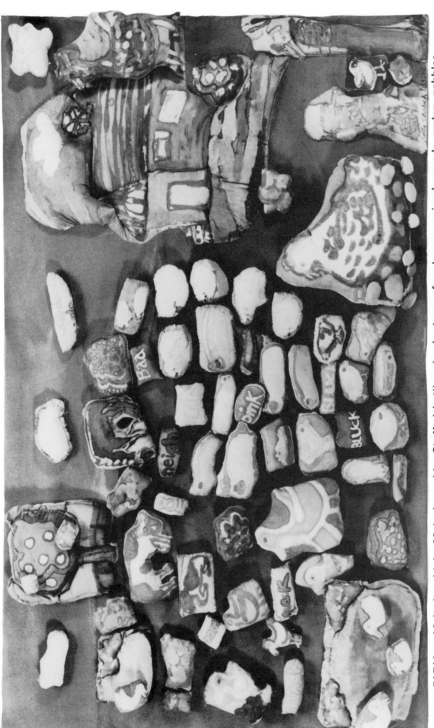

FARM. 40 inches high, 60 inches wide. Stuffed batik animals, trees, farmhouse, animal sounds, water, pebbles, and flowers made with melted Crayola wax on cotton. The background is a piece of cotton stretched over a frame and painted with Liquitex® acrylic paints to give the cloth a stained appearance while still retaining the cloth's softness. The background is painted to resemble the landscape including a pond. Each stuffed piece has snaps sewn on the back which snap to others sewn on the background. They can be unsnapped and moved about the landscape.

Prepared by Binney & Smith, Inc.
Makers of Crayola crayons

PICNIC LUNCH. Kathleen Knipple and Suzanne Mancini. Batiked fabrics on Indian Head cotton are stuffed to simulate real grocery objects. All items are a little larger than actual size. Even the "paper" bag is batiked fabric that is so realistic one has to touch it to believe it is not paper.

Courtesy, artists

9
BATIK PRESENTATION IDEAS

A LENGTH of batiked fabric, beautifully designed and well executed, is a work of art in itself. For countless centuries such fabrics were used for clothing and wall hangings. Little else. Modern artists, discovering innovative applications for batik fabrics, are adding new dimensions to the reasons for creating them. The scores of ideas offered are not meant to be copied, but to stimulate further exploration into the use of textile arts by themselves and in combination with other techniques and media.

Hanging and finishing methods should be observed in all examples. Often curtain rods are placed at tops and bottoms. Fabrics are tacked or glued onto decorative wood moldings. Hanging tabs are planned as part of the batik or compatible material is sewn to top hems. Tassels or braided and knotted fringes are added to straight and scalloped bottom edges. Spring curtain rods are used and hangings are suspended from eyelets in a ceiling.

Picturelike presentations are effective, too. Most popular is to back the fabric with a piece of mat board, then mat and frame the fabric. An inexpensive strip frame, made like a painter's stretcher frame, is another idea; stretch the fabric around the sides of the frame and staple at the back. The fabric itself serves as the frame edge and provides a finished appearance.

Pieces can be preserved and kept dust free by spraying with a plastic coating (Krylon) or brushing on a matte or gloss polymer emulsion (Liquitex). They can be dipped in solutions used for stiffening fabric for window shades (Decor-shade).

When batik fabrics are hung so light comes through them from the back, they have a stained-glass appearance. Hang them in front of windows (not in the sun) by rods suspended from the ceiling or directly on a rod across the window. Vivian Kline frames small pieces of fabric between two sheets of clear plastic (Plexiglas) on a base and places them on a table in front of a window. Some are framed in shadow boxes with a neon tube behind the fabric.

Artists who employ cutout areas admit that the approach usually happened by accident. John Mulder, dissatisfied with one of his large pieces, cut out the successful portions and appliquéd them to a felt background . . . and devised an original approach to solving one problem of the medium.

Batiked fabrics are used in conjunction with other textile techniques including weaving, macramé, reverse appliqué, and stitchery. And when a piece really is considered a failure you can follow Blanche Carstenson's example: cut the fabric into small pieces with pinking shears and adhere them to greeting cards for the ultimate in individualized messages.

RED VOLKSWAGEN. Kathleen Knipple. Stuffed, batiked cotton. Life-size. Old mattresses cut up, polyfoam, cotton, and anything else available was used for stuffing. The doors zip off to reveal a replica of the Volkswagen interior *(below)*.

Courtesy, artist

Kathleen Knipple sits inside her soft sculpture Volkswagen made completely of batiked fabrics.

SPACE HANGING.   Bernice Colman. Batik on silk. The top center portion is stuffed and another dimension is created above the stuffed areas by dribbling polyvinyl chloride (P.V.C.) resin over some of the batiked lines. The piece is framed for hanging.

Courtesy, artist

HANGING.   Lisa Ann Hunter. Quilted batik on silk. 30 inches high, 48 inches wide. Portions of the irregular-shaped piece are quilted. Quilting uses small, undefined stitches to add a textural effect around the shapes.

Courtesy, artist

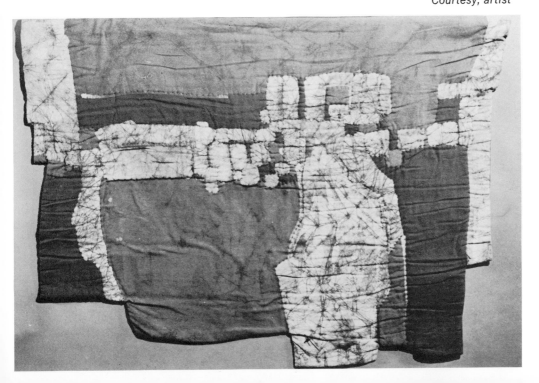

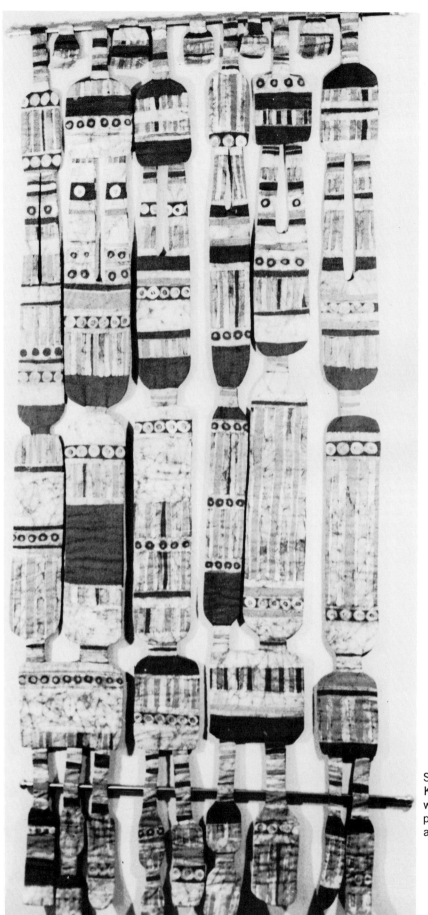

STUFFED HANGING.
Kathleen Knipple. Cotton
with cotton stuffing and
pieces shaped, sewed, and
attached.

Courtesy, artist

SOFT MUSIC.   Carolyn Patterson. Batik on cotton. Batik hanging is combined with soft sculpture shapes dangling from it. Shapes have beads and bells.

Photo, Greg Brown

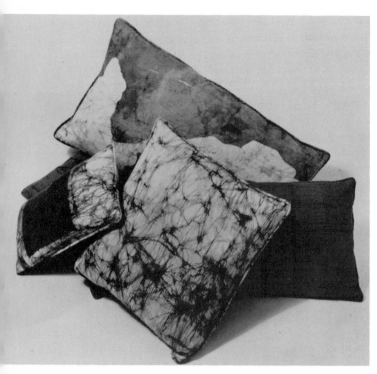

PILLOWS. Jerome Wallace. Utilitarian objects, stuffed, are possibly a forerunner to soft sculpture. But even in pillows, the batiked silk has a richness and individuality characteristic of the technique.

Courtesy, artist

QUILTED BATIK PILLOWS. High school student. The fabric is padded with a layer of Dacron and lining on the back. Stitching brings out the design. The method can be applied to pillows such as these and adapted to all or parts of a wall hanging.

Dacron padding is cut to the fabric shapes, quilted, and then the shapes mounted on a board of another piece of batiked fabric. These shapes were retrieved from a silk batik hanging that had been ruined by dry cleaning.

Quilted pillows in progress: quilting requires the top designed fabric, the Dacron or cotton layer, and a piece of thin fabric for backing. Stitching may be done by hand or machine through all the fabrics. Thread colors may blend or contrast with the design.

WINTER SUNS. John Mulder. Quilted silk batik; Dacron filling and silk lining. 68 inches high, 34 inches wide. Quilting by Phyllis Mulder.

Collection, Mr. & Mrs. Norman Henning,
Oak Park, Ill.

BATIK ON SUEDE. Dolores Ashley-Harris. 12 inches high, 7½ inches wide. Green and brown.

Photo, Joe Zinn

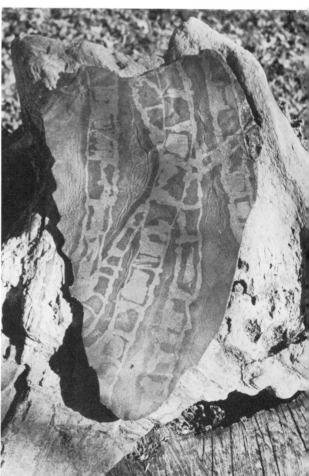

PETROGLADE. Lucille Bealmer. Stuffed velvet quilted hanging with circle of batik on suede. Overall hanging, 32 inches by 32 inches. Circle 22 inches in diameter.

Photo, Steve Terivilliger

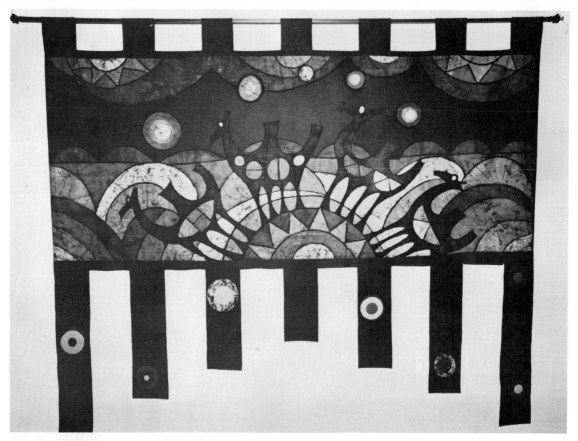

SALT CARAVAN. John Mulder. Batiked Irish linen cut out and appliquéd on green felt. 70 inches high, 85 inches wide. Banner hangs on an adjustable decorative drapery rod.

Detail of above illustrates how the batik shapes are cut out and hand appliquéd by Phyllis Mulder.

REVERSE APPLIQUÉ. Sue Matia-
sevich. Cotton and silk. Two layers
of fabrics are placed together. The
top plain layer is cut out and carefully stitched under to reveal the
bottom batik layer in an interpretation of reverse appliqué . . . a technique attributed to the San Blas
Indians of Panama. This is viewed
with light coming through from the
back.

Detail (above) opaque lighting.
The solid fabric on top is cut out,
hemmed under, and stitched to reveal batik fabric below.

EARTH'S CYCLE.   Carolyn Patterson. Batik with natural
dyes, weaving, and macramé on linen. 40 inch diameter.
Yellows, golds, orchids, and browns. Some natural hand-
spun undyed wool in beiges and whites.
Photo, Greg Brown

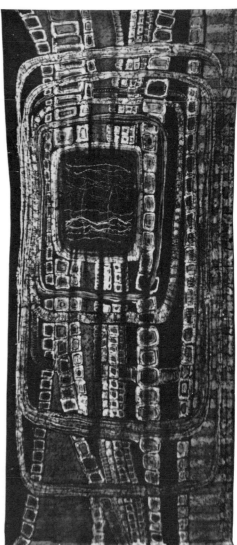

TOCATA.   Bernice Colman. Batik on silk
with inset of twining and lace. 130 inches
high, 42 inches wide.

Courtesy, artist

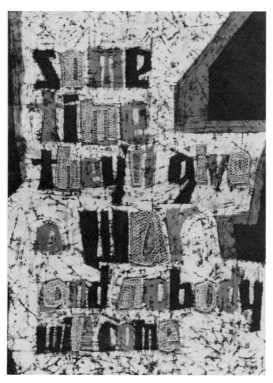

STATEMENT.   Berni Gorski. Batik on
cotton in yellow, orange, and red. 46
inches high, 28 inches wide. Stitches
emphasize letters; an organdy overlay
with stitching is appliquéd in some areas.
Collection, Dr. Derek Price,
New Haven, Conn.

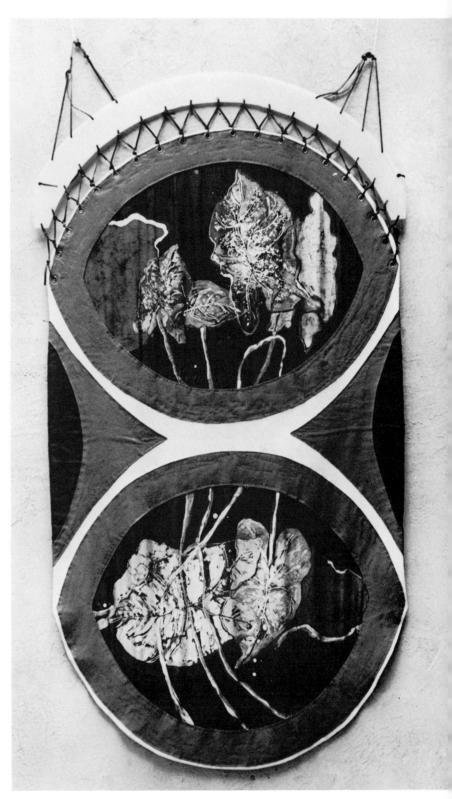

CALADIUMS ONE AND TWO COMBINED. Beth Ford. Batik on silk. Appliqué designs are ocher and white felt and deep purple suede cloth. 8 feet high, 4 feet wide. Curved Plexiglas with leather thongs supports the hanging.
Photo, Judy Durick

SCULPTURAL STONEWARE AND STUFFED BATIK FORMS. Doris C. Petersham. Approximately 18 inches high.

STUFFED BATIK FORMS WITH STONE-WARE. Doris C. Petersham. Batik velveteen shaped like carrots and stuffed have colored yarn for topping. They are placed in a stoneware dish which has the same feeling and colors in the glazes as those in the fabric. Approximately 15 inches high.

I THINKA INCA. Viggo Holm Madsen. Batik on cotton. 36 inches high, 25 inches wide. Tan, rusty reds, ochers, browns, and near-blacks. Says Mr. Madsen: "By accident the fabric tore while being taken off the frame. I continued to tear it until it gave the appearance of an ancient fragment such as a Peruvian sample I had seen in a textile show."

Photo, Thomas Eddy

DUAL LAYER HANGING.   Kathleen Knipple. White and black batik on cotton. Shapes work on two levels and some areas are stuffed. 52 inches high, 10 feet wide.

Courtesy, artist

FANTASY CREATURES.   Patricia Wilson. The arrangement of the figures can be recombined in endless ways to adapt to the demands of different individuals or environments.

Courtesy, artist

COTTON CUTUP. Sharon Lappin-Lumsden. 24 inches high, 18 inches wide. When heavy wax lines remained on an earlier piece, the artist was displeased with them and decided to cut out shapes rather than remove the wax. This piece was purposely planned so the negative spaces would be carefully integrated with the positive shapes. Edges are carefully cut, then sealed with a lightly brushed on coat of white glue to prevent them from fraying.

HANGING.   Lifcha Alper. Batik striped velveteen and silk appliqués are combined and bound, then expanded with strips of suede at edges and bottom. This is another approach to the use of negative space in a hanging.

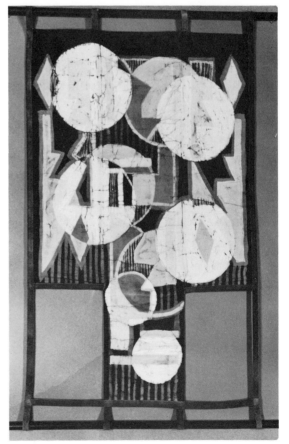

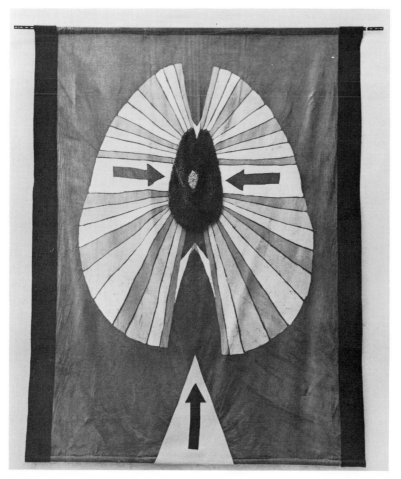

STRIPED TARGET.   Beth Ford. Batik on cotton with fur and felt appliqué. 7 feet high, 5 feet wide. Light purple to hot pink on brownish-purple background. Black felt edge and arrows.

Photo, Judy Durick

EARTH SERIES IV.   Rita Shumaker. Quilted batik with appliqué and stitchery. 40 inches high, 30 inches wide by approximately 1 inch deep. White, yellow, orange, red, rust, fuchsia, wine, and dark brown.

Photo, John Daughtry

AFRICAN IMAGE. Beth Ford. Batik on cotton muslin. 8 feet high, 4 feet wide. White, rusty orange, olive green, and black. Open areas have green yarn wrapped around several threads; pieces of fur are added in center section.
Photo, Judy Durick

SQUARE ROOT. Gene Menger. Batik on heavy weave cotton canvas. After the fabric is dyed, the wax is removed by dry cleaning. The fringed edges are created by unraveling the fabric. Loose areas within, purposely designed, are created by pulling the cross, or weft, threads for an open feeling.

LIPS THAT LOVE TO KISS. Gene Menger. Process same as above.

Photos, courtesy artist

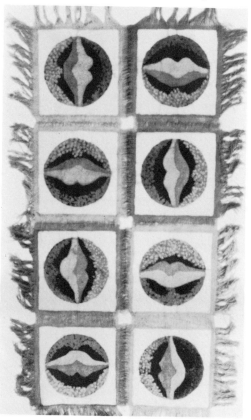

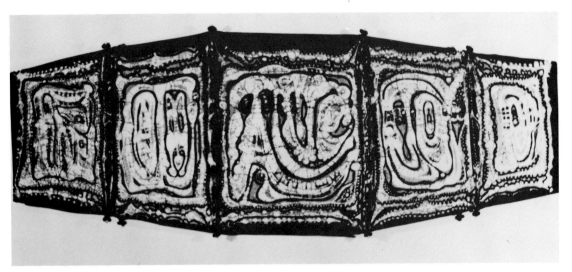

I AM ALIVE.   Lois Brooks. Batik on raw silk. 33 inches high, 7½ feet wide. Textile panel was designed to be stretched over a shaped board. Each section of the design is separated by a raised, drapelike area held tautly at top and bottom by little paw-balls.

Courtesy, artist

BIRD SCREEN.   Marian L. Martin. Three panels were batiked and set into a cut-down frame from a secondhand shoji screen. A fine silk of yellow with lightly crackled brown is used for a lining.

Photo, James R. Pelton

PATCHWORK AFTER THE OLD MASTERS. Dolores Ashley-Harris. When a teacher retains the work of her students, the result, imaginatively assembled, becomes a stunning bedspread.

Photo, Joe Zinn

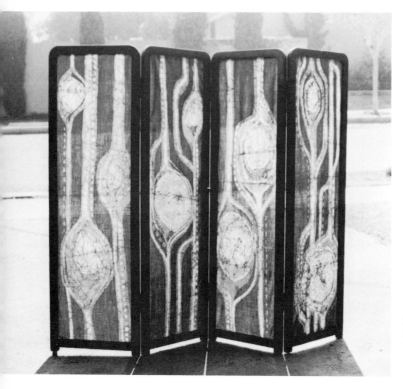

ROOM DIVIDER. Julia George. 36 inches high, 50 inches wide.

Photo, Hermine Daniels

LAMPSHADE WITH BUTTERFLIES. Marian L. Martin. Three panels are glued together and stretched over a wire lampshade frame.

Photo, James R. Pelton

HANGING LAMP. Joyce Stack. The lamp is made so the shade revolves. The placement of the dancer in each panel varies so when the shade revolves the figure appears to be moving.

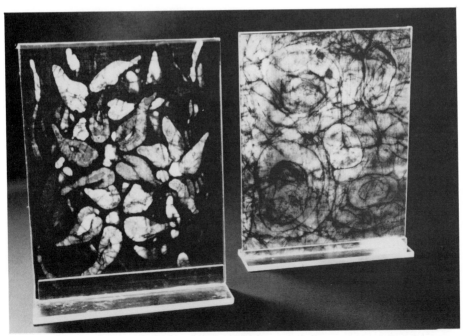

PANELS. Vivian Kline. Plastic frames provide an excellent presentation because they may be placed in front of a window so light comes through the fabric and illuminates the brilliant colors. The artist also mounts some of the fabrics in light boxes.

KITE. Joyce Stack. White, blues, and black on light cotton over a wood kite frame.

FINGER PUPPET (*in progress*). Stephen Blumrich. Design is drawn and batiked on heavy cotton then cut out, allowing a hem which is sewn to a plain cotton backing. The bottom is left open so a hand can be inserted to work the puppet.

ASSORTED FINGER PUPPETS. Stephen Blumrich. All are beautifully crafted and have a minimum of twelve waxings and color dippings.

Special seasons greeting can be designed from batiks. Julia George attaches a mandala to a folded card. Stephen Blumrich makes special puppets for the holidays. Blanche Carstenson uses her scrap pieces of batik, cuts them to shape with pinking shears and attaches them to gift notes *(not shown)*.

STUFFED DOLL. Candace Johnson. Fabrics are cut to shape, then batiked, stuffed, and sewn. Always use good, strong fabric for such pieces, as the amount of tugging and pulling required when stuffing will readily tear a thin fabric. Stuff with cotton, old hosiery, Dacron, or polyfoam particles.

STUFFED ANIMALS. Stephen Blumrich. You can design your own animal shapes. Patterns for these are available from sewing pattern books: the same as those used for calico animals can be used to design batik "skins."

THE FISH STRINGER. Elizabeth Fuller. Stuffed fish on a fabric string would be fun for any tomboy to bring home. No worms needed. Only wax.

DOLL QUILT. Elizabeth Fuller. Batik, appliqué, and quilting are combined in this small quilt used as a hanging.

Courtesy, artist

Batik Easter eggs in the Ukrainian style by Ilona Bodo.

10

BATIK EGGS

A DISCUSSION of batik would be incomplete without examples of Ukrainian Easter eggs. In A.D. 988 when the Ukraine accepted Christianity, the decorated Easter egg became an important symbol in the ritual of the new religion. The technique shown is called "pysanka"; coloring raw eggs by waxing and dipping them in colors. They are not made to be eaten. They do not rot or deteriorate. No two pysanky eggs are decorated exactly alike, but all contain well-known iconographic symbols that are deeply implanted in the religion of the people. Such symbols include the star, which is believed to have been the symbol of the pagan sun god Atar. Crossed lines drawn within the shapes of diamonds and triangles symbolize any trio such as the Holy Trinity; fire, air, water; three stages of man, and so forth.

The basic design of the egg is developed by dividing the surface into sections, or fields, with lines running perpendicularly and/or horizontally around the egg. Many divisions are planned to separate individual motifs.

Anyone creating a pysanka egg today may organize the design by dividing it into sections, then using the technique in a free style to explore this ancient folk art in a new direction. There are two methods of decorating the eggs: 1) use the traditional batik method of waxing and dipping in dyes as illustrated, or 2) first dip the egg in a colored dye and then paint melted colored wax directly for the design; colors and wax remain on the egg. Some people prefer to blow out the egg from the shell before coloring and then to plug the hole with wax.

Materials needed are a candle, a "kistka," which is a special stylus (a tjanting or brush may be used), rubber band, beeswax, egg holder, and dyes dissolved in water. The egg should be white, smooth, raw, and preferably farm fresh. Commercially cleaned eggs often show scratches when dried. Wash egg in warm water mixed with a tablespoon of white vinegar. Colors used for dipping are yellow, orange, and red. Blue will be added over the yellow to achieve some green areas.

Place a wide rubber band lengthwise around the egg to divide it down the middle. Place wax on the kistka or other tool you are using. (You can sketch a design lightly with pencil but don't erase the pencil marks as this will scratch the egg.)

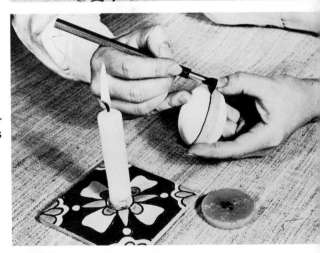

Draw a line in wax along both edges of the rubber band, always holding the egg very carefully so as not to squeeze it or drop it.

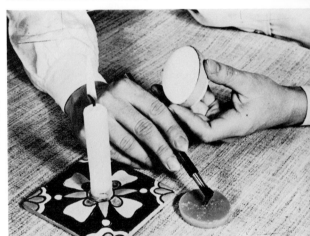

When both lines are drawn lift the band gently and remove it, being careful not to break the wax lines. Once the wax has been applied to the egg it cannot be taken off or erased.

Continue to draw lines with the wax until the sections of the egg are filled in where you wish to retain white areas of the egg.

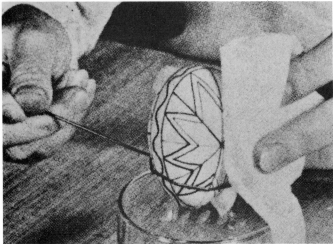

Dip the egg in the first and lightest color, yellow. Allow the egg to remain in the dye until the desired shade is reached. Remove and pat dry with soft cloth or tissues.

You can add dye color directly with a small paintbrush or toothpick. An area of blue dye added over the yellow will turn green. Dry and wax over the green to hold it from subsequent dippings.

Let the egg dry. Wax the lines that you wish to remain yellow in your final design. The petals' outline will be yellow.

The egg is dipped into the second color, in this case orange. Further waxing is done over the portions you wish to remain orange.

After the egg has been placed in the third dye color (red), cover the remaining un-waxed red portions with wax also so that the entire egg has a waxing.

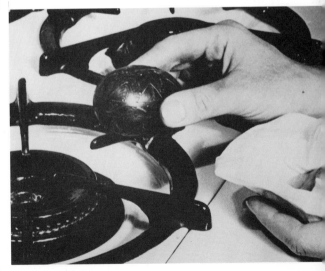

To remove wax, hold egg over the edge of a gas flame. As small areas begin to melt, wipe with clean tissues. Rotate and repeat until all wax is removed. Or, place egg on a tissue in an oven at 250° for a few minutes. When wax begins to shine remove egg and wipe with tissues. When dry, gloss with a coating of plastic spray or a thin, clear shellac applied with a lint-free cloth.

All photos, courtesy, Surma Book & Music Co., New York

Two Ukrainian pysanky Easter eggs decorated by the wax batik method.

Collection: Dona Meilach

Tied gathers and circles are used in the yardage. The design in the leotard is made by clamping a cutout wood shape into the material and then dyeing. Virginia Belone.

Courtesy, Red Rock Tie Dye and CPC International, Inc.

11

TIE-DYE AND ITS VARIATIONS

IN batik, areas of fabric are resisted by covering them with wax. In tie-dye, areas of the fabric are resisted by tying, folding, stitching, and clamping. The type of tie, the direction and spacing of the tying cord, the manner in which the material is folded, stitched, or clamped, and the number of color dippings all contribute to the design.

Basically, the procedure for tie-dye is:

1. Prepare the fabric and plan the design.
2. Tie, fold, stitch, or clamp the fabric.
3. Dye and rinse the fabric.
4. Retie or overtie and redye for subsequent colors.
5. Untie and iron the fabric.

Fabrics used for tie-dye are the natural fibers used for batik: cotton, linen, silk, and wool. They must be washed to remove sizing. Synthetic fabrics are not as receptive to the majority of dyes recommended. Some people prefer to mordant natural fabric before dyeing. Mordant, from the French word, "to bite," involves soaking the fabric in a chemical solution (see appendix for formulas) to make the fibers more receptive to the dyes. Fabrics should be tied before they are mordanted so they can go directly into the dyebath. Mordanting is not essential.

Plastic, enamel, or glass vessels should be large enough to accommodate the fabric in ample solution to cover. Fabrics should be wet out before dyeing, following the same procedures as for batik, chapter 14.

Dyes used for tie-dye can be hot water dyes as well as cold water dyes. If you are using waxed cords or combining tie-dye with batik, then use only cold water dyes: household dyes may also be used at lower temperatures (consult chapter 14). When using fiber reactive cold water dyes, resist areas must be exceptionally well tied, preferably with waxed cords or rubber bands, and thoroughly dried before untying so the wet dyes do not continue to migrate into the undyed areas.

Perhaps the greatest fun for the beginning tie-dyer is seeing the designs that result when fabrics are tied in different ways. For samplers, tear old sheets into small squares and practice each tie to understand how it works. After you make a few of each kind of tie, you can recognize the result in a finished piece and emulate the general design.

The various ties can be easily categorized and they are presented in this order: overall patterns, circles, gathering, folding, clamping, wrapping in objects, and stitching. Involved patterns are simply variations and combinations of the basic ties.

The tie cord used and its placement on the fabric determine the character of the resist line. Experiment with various types of cords on one piece of fabric and dye it to observe the results. If a tie material is wide, such as a thick·rubber band or piece of elastic, the area that will remain white will be as wide as the tie. Cords tied slightly apart will result in lines with color between as the dye creeps between the cords. Wrappings that are very tight from top to bottom will yield sharp lines; if top and bottom wraps are slightly loose, a soft muted line is likely.

Select cords for binding that will not break easily as they are subjected to severe pulling. Use buttonhole and carpet thread, fishing line, seine twine, elastic, rope, dental floss, waxed string, rubber bands, strips of material, masking tape, wire, and plastic wrap. For holding folds and creating spotted areas employ clothespins, bulldog clips, paper clips, and large bobby pins.

When tying, allow a long end at beginning and end of the tie to facilitate locating the ends when you want to untie. Make double knots, but make one loose enough so you can get the point of a pair of scissors beneath without tearing the fabric. For cutting use seam rippers, nail scissors, blunt point scissors, or an X-acto knife.

Ties can be dyed in colors first and used for binding; the tie colors will tend to bleed into the fabric during the dye procedures and result in a subtle combination of colors that bleed into one another.

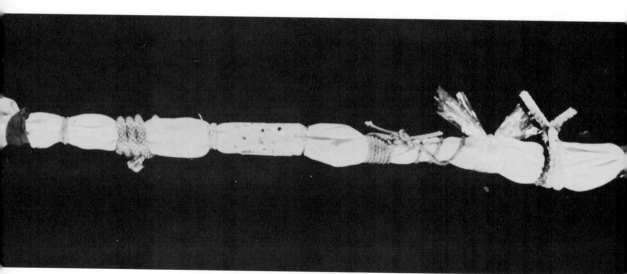

TIE MATERIAL USED (*left to right*)
Wide rubber band, thin rubber band, nylon rope, gold bead wire, masking tape with holes poked into it, cotton rope, Saran wrap, colored cord, pipe cleaners, rubber bands.

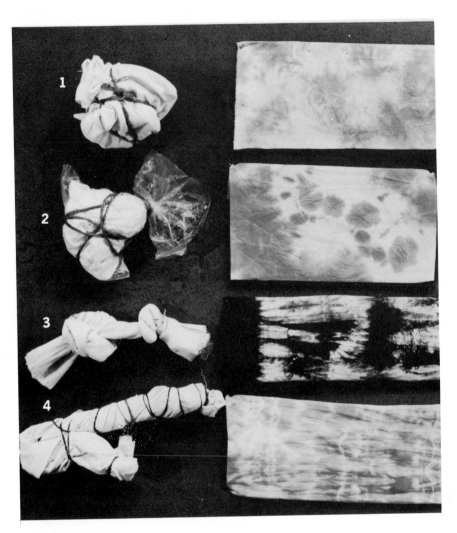

OVERALL PATTERNS

Four methods for creating overall tie-dyed patterns are shown, top to bottom.

1. *Marbleizing.* Scrunch up the fabric, tie tightly in random fashion with cords or rubber bands. Dye, rinse, dry, and open.

2. *Marbleizing and spotting* through a plastic bag. Bunch the cloth and twist it, and place inside first one plastic bag, and then another, twisting the necks so dye cannot enter. Tie around with cord or rubber bands. Then poke pin holes through both bags to let dye seep in. The result is shown. Placing the fabric inside a nylon stocking or a mesh bag, then tying, will also result in an overall pattern. Patterns created can be retied in other areas and redyed a second color.

3. *Overhand knotting* will give the effect shown at right. Make knots close together or far apart.

4. *Twisting.* Gather a length of fabric and hold one end tight while twisting the other until the length twists back on itself. Then tie it and dye for allover pattern that can be used as a background for additional tie designs.

CIRCULAR SHAPES

A *single rosette circle* is made by (1) pinching up a spot on the fabric, then dropping the material all around and tying it any distance down. Only the portion that is tied will resist the dyed color. (2) By continuing to tie all the way down, a series of concentric circles will result in a sunburst pattern. Keep the tie cord continuous for a random series of circles as shown; if each bound section is tied off with individual rubber bands or cords, the circular lines will be sharp, more distinct, and disconnected.

The donut; a circle within a circle. (1) Pick a point on the fabric, hold it with two fingers, and allow the rest of the fabric to drop over your hand. Gather the material and tie as in (2), catching the point within the tie also. (3) The piece with the point tucked within is tied. Often very amoeboid shapes will result.

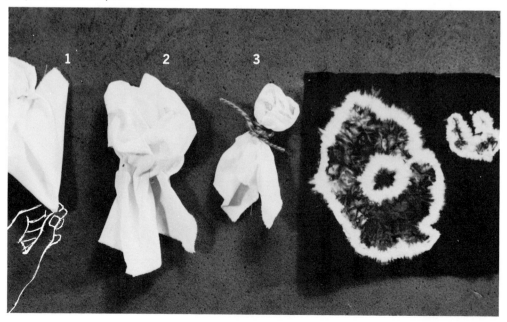

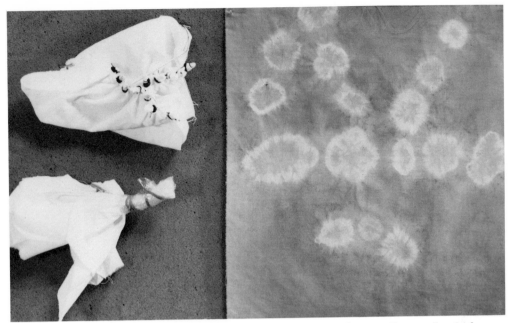

Spots (top right) are made by binding up small rosette areas in a continuous line to form a triangle, circle, curve, or any shape grouping. For a dotted effect in the spots, bind with plastic wrap and poke holes in the wrap. Diamond shape spots are tied the same way but the fabric is pulled on the cross of the cloth.

Sunbursts and spots are arranged symmetrically. The fabric was first folded into sections the desired width for the sunbursts, then the spots were made along the fold. For two colors, tie the first set of spots, dye; untie and retie for dyeing over the original spots. Thomas Lamarr Brigman.

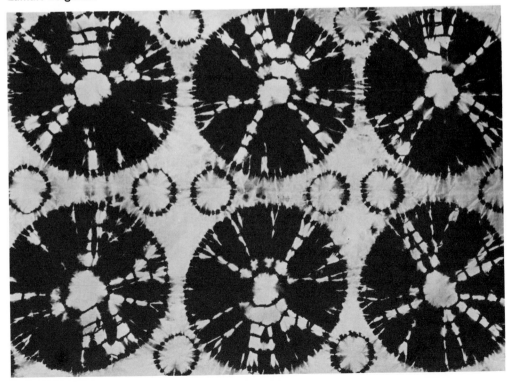

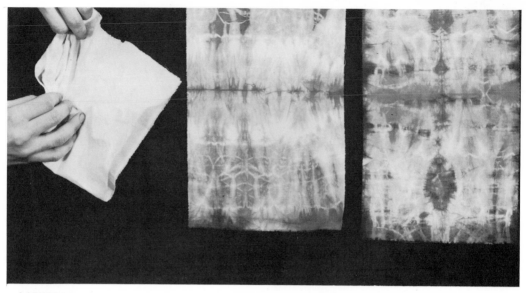

GATHERING

Gathering can be used for making an entire background area of muted stripes or for single narrow stripes. Simply gather the fabric as shown and tie up in the same way as the sunburst (page 183) is tied . . . using one cord up and down the tie.

A gathered stripe on each side of diamond shape spots. Diamonds are made by tying as for spots, then pulling the tie on the cross of the fabric. Thomas Lamarr Brigman (detail)

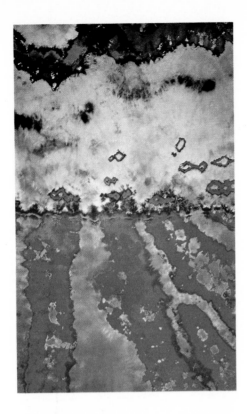

RED HORIZON. Marian Clayden. Silk panel using tritik and discharge dye techniques. 5 ft. 8 in. high, 3½ ft. wide.   *Courtesy, artist*

MEDITATION TENT. Marian Clayden. Environmental tie-dye using tritik and discharge dye techniques on silk. 5 ft. high, 6½ ft. diam.
Courtesy, artist

Tie-dye chiffon yardage.
Courtesy, CPC International

THE SUMMER GARDEN. Quinja and Multifarious Maya. A room planned as a complete tie-dyed environment using velvet and silk for the walls, canvas for the floors, and a soft silk air sculpture sky. Eighty-five yards of velvet, fifty-four yards of silk, and thirty-four yards of canvas were used.
Collection, Mrs. C. F. Murphy, Jr., Chicago

Tie-dyed clothing of cottons and silks. Courtesy, CPC International

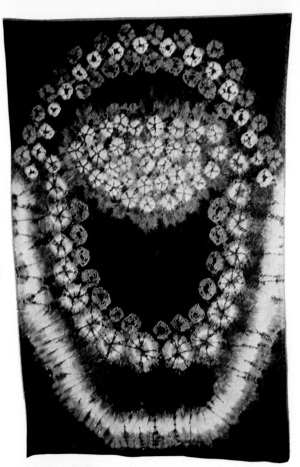

RADIANCE. Bernice Colman. Tie-dye on velvet. 50 in. high, 31 in. wide.   *Courtesy, artist*

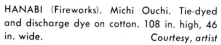

HANABI (Fireworks). Michi Ouchi. Tie-dyed and discharge dye on cotton. 108 in. high, 46 in. wide.   *Courtesy, artist*

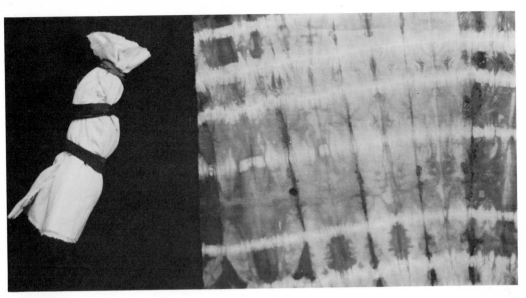

PLEATING

Pleating is a variation of gathering. The fabric is carefully accordian-folded and tied with a continuous cord up and down for muted stripes. For definite stripes, make individual ties at desired distances apart on the folded fabric. Resulting lines will be clean-cut stripes. The difference between overall muted horizontals with connecting lines and carefully controlled separated lines is only this difference in placing and tying the cords.

Example of a pleated and tied stripe with gathering at top and bottom. The fabric was folded in half and then pleated to result in the double reverse image. David Berglund (detail)

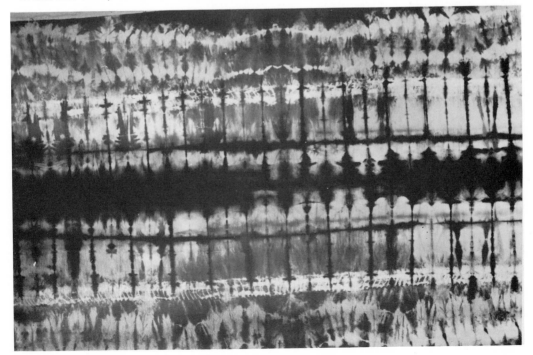

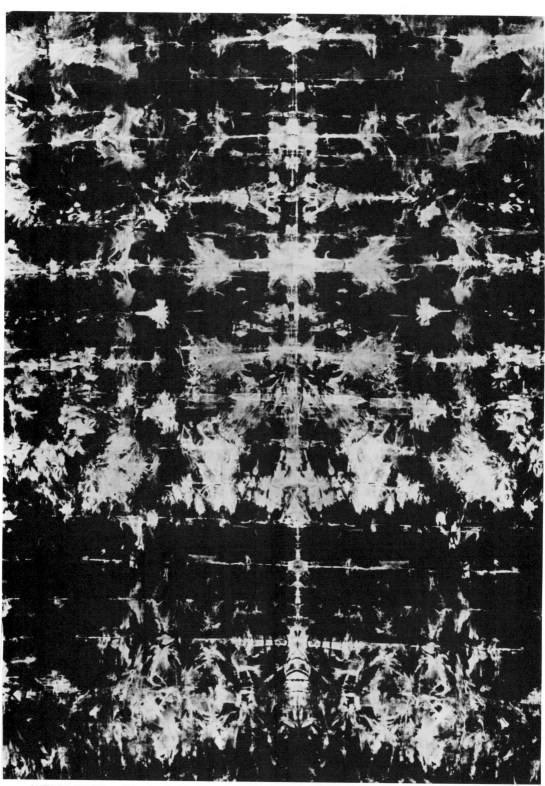

INTEGRATION. Rita L. Shumaker. Detail of length of 4 yard fabric in black and white discharge made by pleating and tying.

Photo, John Daughtry

WATERSPRITES. Rita L. Shumaker. 48 inches long, 44 inches wide. Sunbursts, gathering, spots, rosettes, and some stitching. Notice that gathered areas are curved around the sunburst, as well as making horizontals. Blue and brown on white batiste.

Photo, John Daughtry

FOLDING IDEAS

There are, literally, hundreds of ways to fold fabrics to achieve exciting results with dyes. Once you attempt a few folds, hold them together, or tie them up and dye them, you'll have a better understanding of how the colors penetrate the fabrics and spread out to form designs. Thinner fabrics are suggested when multiple folding is planned. It's a good idea to practice on paper for folding techniques because it is stiffer than fabric and less expensive. Paper and fabrics can be folded and not tied for brilliant effects: the dyes can be applied directly to the folds and the paper or fabric squeezed in the same manner as a Rorschach inkblot.

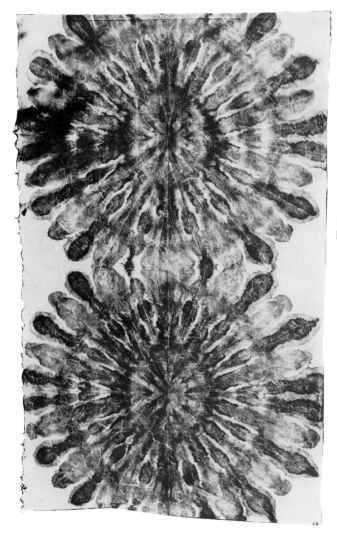

Folded sunbursts on a rice paper hanging. Pat Shipley and Pat Lazier. *Collection, Doris Hoover*

Folded paper utilizes an off-center design arrangement by Pat Shipley and Pat Lazier on heavy, textured rice paper. Paper can be both dipped in color and colors added with an eyedropper or meat baster; then the paper squeezed. Overdyeing can be accomplished by using additional colors when the first ones dry.

Collection, Doris Hoover

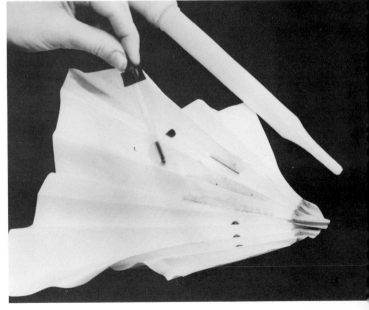

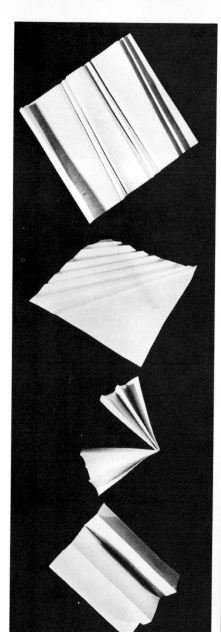

Practicing folds on paper will help you visualize how to work them out in fabric. When multi-folding fabrics it helps to iron the pleats in and use pins, if necessary, so they will hold as you continue to fold and then tie.

A folded and tied bundle of fabric is dropped into a dyebath.

CHEVRONS AND DIAMONDS (detail).
Charlotte White. Fold-dye silk. White, blue,
turquoise, brown, purple, and white. Diagonal lines occur when the fabric is folded on
angles.

Drawing illustrates the folding for CHEV-
RONS AND DIAMONDS above. The fabric is
folded horizontally and then folded on angles
indicated by the dotted lines. The folds are
made as in accordian pleating using straight
pins to hold them in place. The pins are removed as the fabric is tied. For each color,
ties are changed along the folds but the
folds remain constant.

Courtesy, artist

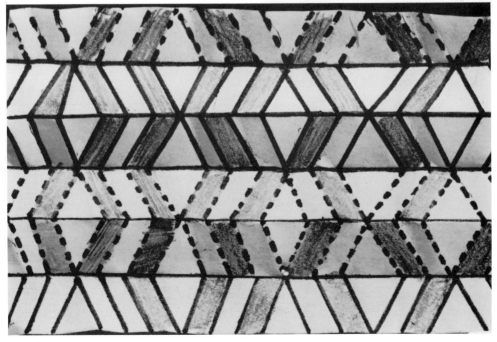

SAMPLERS.   Grace Earl. *(Left)* Fold-dye and discharge result in brown and navy on black cotton broadcloth. *(Right)* Discharge fold and tie-dye.

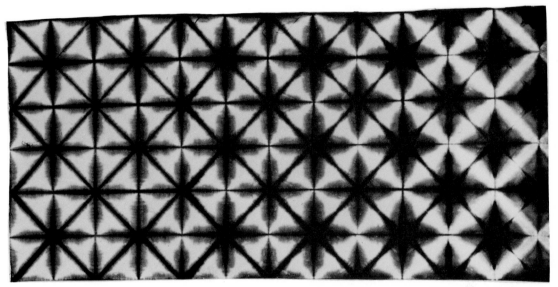

Folds, not tied, can be immersed in dyebath so only the edges are dyed and create a pattern as the dye creeps into the fabric, heavier at the folds and undyed in the centers. Many overdyes can be created by refolding and redyeing only some of the corners. Jane Dimiceli.

Collection, Grace Earl

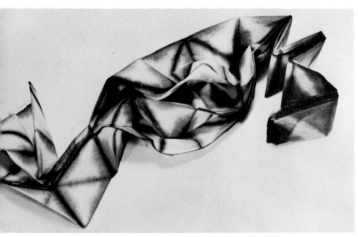

The fabric folded.

Edges are dipped into the dye.

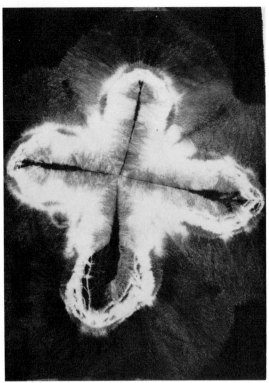

HOW TO FOLD-DYE A CROSS

Folding and tying a cross is demonstrated by Quinja Maya on a rectangular piece of cloth. Experiment with a small sample before dyeing a large piece of fabric. This cross is red and purple on white velveteen.

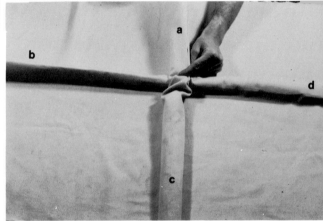

Draw a light line or determine the four "arms" of the cross by making a 1-inch-wide fold crosswise from the center for the length of each arm.

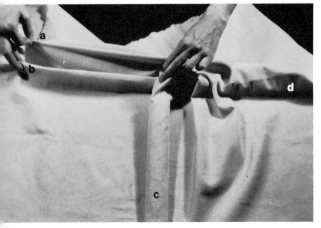

Hold the center of the cross with one hand and with the other hand pick up the tip of arm **a** and bring it to the tip of arm **b.**

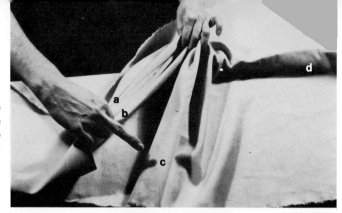

Still holding the center bring the two folds to the tip of arm **c.** Now take the three folds and pick up arm **d.** Hold so the finished four folds are shaped like a triangle.

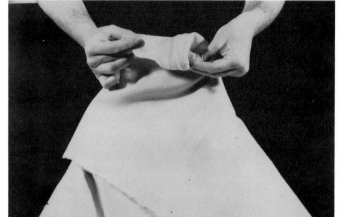

Take the point of the triangle and roll from the center down to about the size you wish the first color of the cross to be.

Tie tightly with elastic or hold with heavy rubber bands.

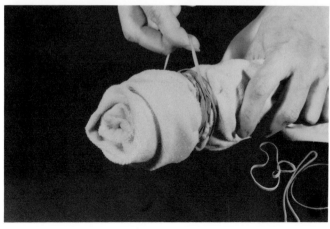

It will look like this when finished. Dye. For the second color add more ties below the first and redye.

FOLD-DYE A SQUARE

A square consisting of squares within can be made by folding the cloth carefully, following the diagrams shown. After the folding is completed, bind the folded cloth with individual ties so the lines will be sharply delineated. If you wish the center to remain the original color of the cloth, bind off the tip of the square tightly. For multiple colors, add bindings after each dipping, but always retain your original bindings if you want to retain the white areas. Thin fabrics such as silk, chiffon, and batiste work well for multiple folding because the dyes can penetrate more thoroughly than in thick fabrics.

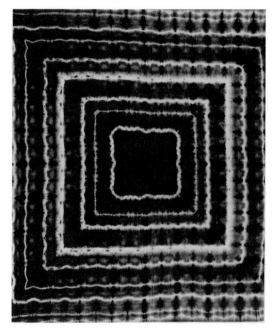

SQUARES. David Berglund. Silk. 48 inches square.

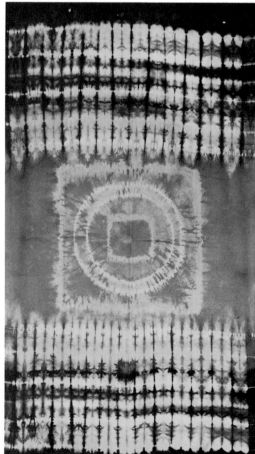

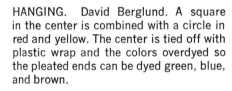

HANGING. David Berglund. A square in the center is combined with a circle in red and yellow. The center is tied off with plastic wrap and the colors overdyed so the pleated ends can be dyed green, blue, and brown.

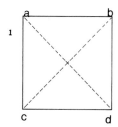
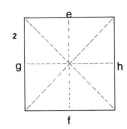
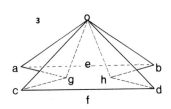

1. Practice the fold on a paper towel and then on fabric. Begin with a perfect square;
Fold **a** to **d**. Unfold
Fold **b** to **c**. Unfold
2. Fold at line **g-h.** Unfold. Fold at line **e-f.** Unfold.
3. Hold at center, point **o,** and arrange as illustrated . . .

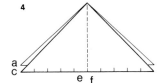
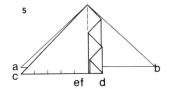
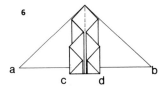

4. . . . making a perfect triangle with point **g-h** inside and meeting under point **e-f.** Measure and mark off evenly along bottom line.
5. Fold corner **d** into folds as shown, using the measured markings as your folding guide.
6. Do the same with point **c,** being sure that all corners of folds meet. This is the secret for making perfect squares.

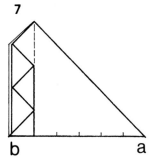
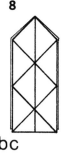

7. Turn the triangle over and measure and fold in corner **b** to center line.
8. Measure and fold in corner **a** so that you have all four corners folded as illustrated.
9. Tie, as desired. The tied areas will resist color; the untied areas will remain white. (You can bleach tip or dip in darker colors.)

SUMMER FLOWER. Michi Ouchi. Multicolor on white cotton broadcloth, using dyes and bleach. 36 inches high, 27 inches wide. The folds are accordion pleated from the center out to each end, then tied and dyed.

Courtesy, artist

FESTIVAL BANNER. Pat Nichelson. A fold dye can be a simple stark statement.
Courtesy, Mint Museum of Art,
Charlotte, N.C.

FOLD DYE *(detail).* Pat Nichelson. Or it can be a large abstract shape made by doubling the material, folding, dipping edges, and overdyeing.

CLAMPING

Unusual, exciting patterns can be created by applying pressure to areas of folded cloth. Pressure can be applied using C-clamps with objects between them; then the fabric is dipped into the dyebath or dye is shot into the fabric with an eyedropper or baster, as shown. Shaped pieces of wood can be used for specific designs (*see* the following series). Objects such as gears, washers, coins, marbles, and pieces of wire screen can be clamped between the boards for a wide array of shapes. Experiment with samples of fabric until you get the feeling of how different items used between the clamps affect the pattern. If a metallic article rusts, or oxidizes, when it is placed in the dye, this rust color can creep into the fabric for an interesting touch of color. You can also place pieces of colored fabric, strings, and art paper between the folds so the additional colors will bleed into the fabric when it is placed in the dyebath.

The fabric is folded and clamped between two pieces of wood.

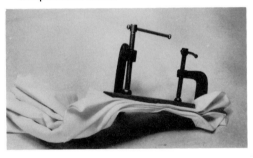

The edges are dipped into dye.

The result.

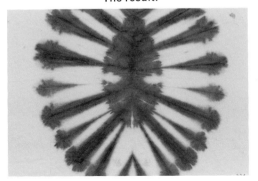

It can be refolded and reclamped and additional colors shot into the folds.

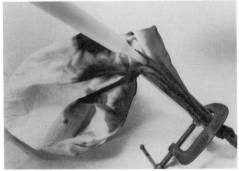

DESIGNS FROM STENCIL BLOCKS

The clamping technique has many possible variations. Will and Eileen Richardson designed an entire line of exciting designs on cloth for the Rit Dye Company using clamps and cutwood stencils. Combinations of wood stencil blocks with curved or straight lines can be designed and applied to fabric yardage, wall hangings, and clothing. They can be used on cut pattern parts or on garments already sewed together.

Two blocks of plywood are cut to shape with a saw and the fabrics placed between them as illustrated in the following demonstrations. Colors for the stencil block and stripes are applied directly from a squeeze bottle or an eyedropper. These parts are resisted when the fabric is immersed in dye for the background color. Stencils can be cut any shape: hearts, diamonds, initials, abstracts, free forms. You can use precut pieces of wood such as Tinkertoy parts and shapes from children's building blocks.

Photo series, courtesy CPC International, Inc.
Drawings and design, courtesy Will and Eileen Richardson

Shirt decorated with a rain cloud pattern in Evening Blue using a wood stencil. Curve pattern is a stripe each of yellow, tangerine, and green.

General procedures for decorating the white shirt can be seen in the drawings and then in the photos on the following pages.

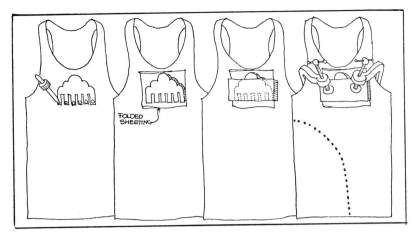

DRAWINGS

The shirt is washed thoroughly, wrung out to remove excess moisture, and sandwiched between 2 stencil blocks. Color is added with an eyedropper under the clamped block at the top of the rain cloud stencil. A small piece of sheet is folded to protect the top of the rain cloud. Then another block of wood is placed under and over the shirt front; all are clamped together. For a slightly different effect, color can be squeezed under after the clamp is in place.

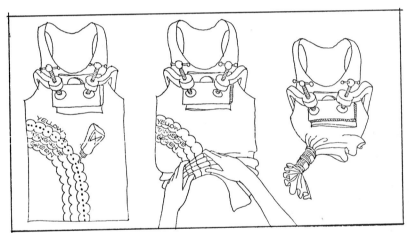

Three colors are squirted along a curve and worked in with the fingers. The fabric is gathered along the curve and tied, then wrapped with plastic to protect it from being overdyed with the background color.

The shirt before it is dipped into the overall background color.

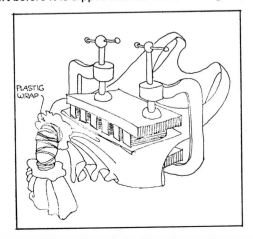

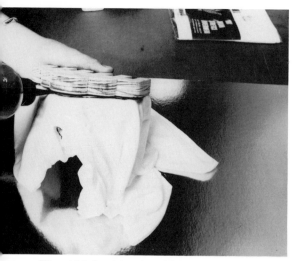

The shirt front is placed between the two rain-cloud pattern wood stencil blocks. The top wood rain cloud is lifted slightly and a drop of Evening Blue is placed at the bottom of each raindrop. Cover the cloud area with 3 or 4 layers of folded sheeting and replace rain cloud. (See drawing, page 201.)

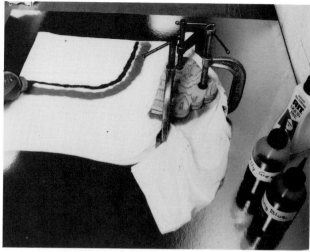

Clamp the two wood blocks with the sheeting and shirt sandwiched between them using C-clamps. Make sure blocks do not slip out of position. Keep clamps from crushing and folding excess fabric. If the blocks are uneven or you are using more than one piece of wood for patterns, place a flat rectangle of wood over each at top and bottom to hold the pattern (as shown in the drawing on the previous page).

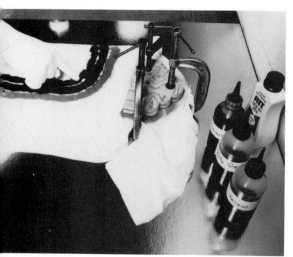

Draw a curved line from 2 inches below arm to center of hem. Apply colors with squeeze bottle (above) then work in with fingers until each stripe is about 1 inch wide. Colors used are Rit liquid yellow, tangerine, and green. (Green is mixed using 1 tablespoon of Evening Blue with 2 tablespoons of yellow.)

Gather shirt along the curve in 1-inch pleats.

Tightly wind rubber bands around the yellow, then the green, and finally the tangerine stripes. Cover the banded area with plastic wrap and fasten tightly with rubber bands to make the area waterproof and resist the purple background color.

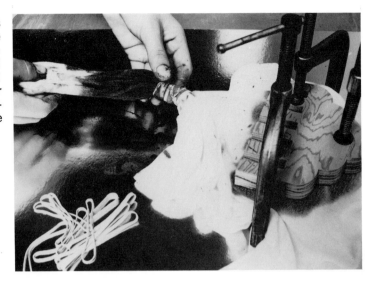

Dissolve half a bottle of purple liquid dye in a large pot of hot water. Submerge shirt, clamps, wood, and all. Simmer one hour and stir frequently.

Remove and rinse in cold running water until water runs clear. Untie curve area first and rinse thoroughly again. Unclamp and rinse rain-cloud area.

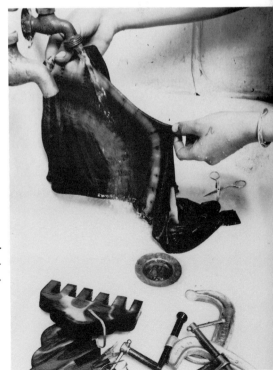

Tying objects into the fabric before dyeing can create infinite variety. Pat Obye ties in different-sized round shapes, including fishing bobbers, Ping-Pong balls and rubber balls. The folds that result between the tied areas also heighten pattern interest.

Courtesy, artist

TYING IN OBJECTS

Fascinating patterns can be achieved in a tie-dyed fabric by tying in objects from very tiny corn kernels and rice to large fishing floats and orange juice cans. Unique motifs result from tying in marbles, popcorn, stones, drapery rings, corks, chunks of wood in free form and definite shapes, Tinkertoy parts, sticks, drawer and doorknobs, thread spools, hair rollers, hardware items including different-sized washers, nuts, and bolts, and anything you can think of that will create a shape.

Often a piece of wood used for several dyeings will absorb color and then discharge it into fabric on subsequent dippings. Tie colored art tissue paper and felt in, too, for color bleeding. You can rub *Crayolas* over the fabric before dyeing, then tie in the object, and the *Crayola* color will discharge in the area. Metal objects will often discharge their own oxidized coloration into the fabric for additional dye tones.

Pattern interest depends on the shape of the object, how it is tied and arranged. The fabric with the object tied in should be wet out before immersing in dye.

A grouping of marbles is tied into a fabric. Some are individually tied in with thin rubber bands and then the entire clump is held with a wide rubber band.

The resulting pattern from each of four marbles tied separately and the larger rings from the overall tie.

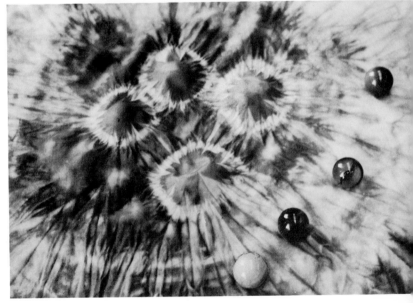

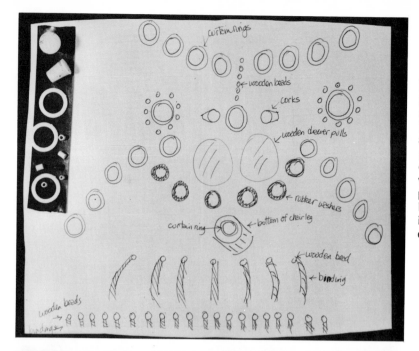

Hallie Redman carefully plans her design on paper and determines the objects that will be tied in and where. For this composition she uses plastic curtain rings, rubber washers, corks, drawer pulls, wooden beads, and long binding over rosettes in the doubled sheer silk chiffon material.

The fabric is folded in half and tied according to the pattern.

Close-up showing bindings with beads at end, drawer pulls, plastic rings, and rubber washers.

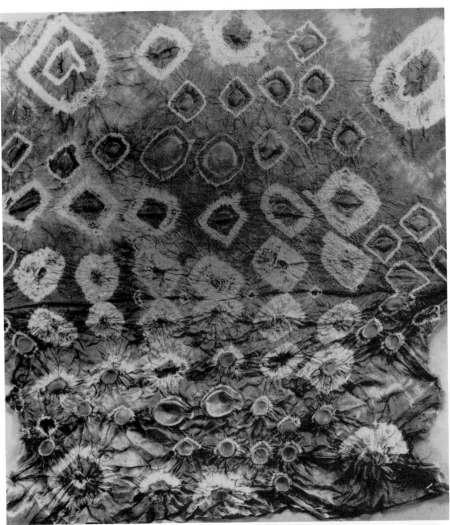

PUCKER UP. Hallie Redman. Tie-dye on silk chiffon showing one half stretched and the other half puckered.

TABLECLOTH. Sharon Meeker. Small circles in a repeat pattern are made by tying in popcorn kernels.

Courtest, artist

STITCHING OR TRITIK

The stitching, or tritik, resist consists of drawing up a thread sewn into the fabric so the puckers or folds that result resist the dye. Very intricate and controlled designs can be developed by this method.

The principle is simple. Any pattern, whether a straight line, curve, spiral, diamond, square, or combination can be drawn and then outlined by stitching with string or thread. When the stitching is pulled tight, the fabric puckers and creates folds. A number of rows can be stitched; designs can cross over one another; they can be regular or irregular. The fabric can be used in single layers or doubled over.

Sturdy threads and good-size needles should be used. The sewn threads are subjected to pulling and, if they are weak, they will break after you have done so much work. Nylon fishing line, waxed thread, buttonhole and carpet thread are strong and suitable.

The main rule to follow is always to knot the thread at each end and leave extra length for grabbing it and pulling it from both sides. When pulling, you can gradually slide the cloth along the thread until it is bunched up. After pulling, tie the two ends of the thread together securely so the gathered fabric does not come apart while it is in the dyebath.

The most popular stitches used are the running stitch and the whipping stitch. For the running stitch, simply place the needle in and out. The whipping stitch is done over a hem or over a fold of the fabric and is shown in the photos that follow.

You can sew several rows of stitches, pull up some to resist the first dyeing, and then tighten others to resist subsequent dyebaths. Variations occur if some of the first rows are released to receive later color. Experiment with samples, as shown, and label them after dyeing so you'll know which stitch and direction resulted in which pattern.

Stitching methods are also used on dark fabrics where discharge patterns are desired.

Right
A velveteen square tied and stitched. Safety pins mark the beginning and ends of stitches, which are often hard to find after they are pulled up and dyed. Safety pins can also be used instead of stitching to gather folded materials and hold them. A resist line will result if the fabric is on the pin tightly. Notice the knots made in the ends of the stitched cords. Running stitches may be used on a single or double layer of fabric. This piece was tied and dyed one color. Cords will be pulled up for subsequent colors. Grace Earl.

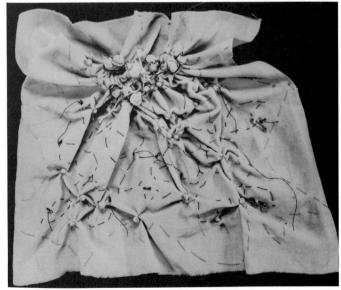

Left
Stitching combined with tied clusters of circles creates a pattern in the undyed piece of raw silk. Jim Bassler.

Courtesy, artist

Running stitches made in various patterns will yield diamonds and circle shapes. At *left:* a stitched fabric sampler with the threads pulled tightly. Grace Earl.

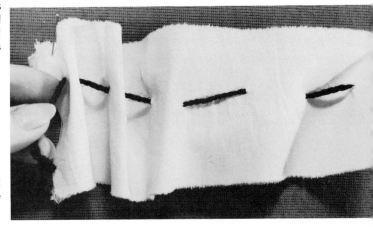

To gather, hold the knot at one end and push the fabric up along the stitches. Tie ends together.

The whipping stitch made over a fold.

A sampler of stitches and tied circles. Grace Earl. The tiny vertebrae-like patterns separating each square are made with a tiny whipping stitch over the folded fabric.

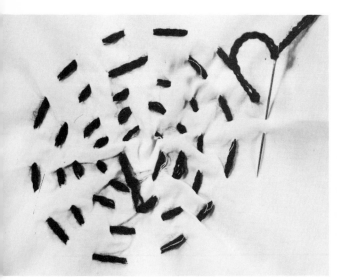

A running stitch—sewed in cotton velveteen in a spiral pattern—will appear like this after it is pulled up, bound, and dyed. Grace Earl.

A combination of rows of running stitches with stitches over it . . .

. . . . will result in a pattern like this. Grace Earl.

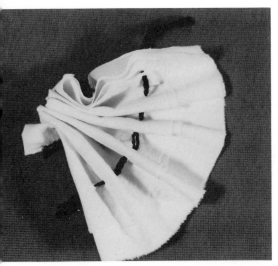

A curved stitch on a piece of folded fabric can produce a lovely, simple design . . .

DISTENDED GESTURE. Clinton D. MacKenzie.

Courtesy, artist

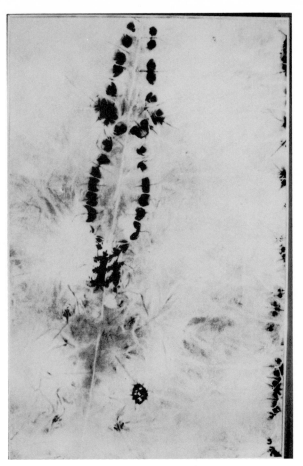

The folded fabric is whipstitched so a curve results.

WHISPERED GESTURE. Clinton D. MacKenzie. 34 inches high, 22 inches wide. Framed velour discharge panel made by folding and sewing the fabric in a curved line.

Courtesy, artist

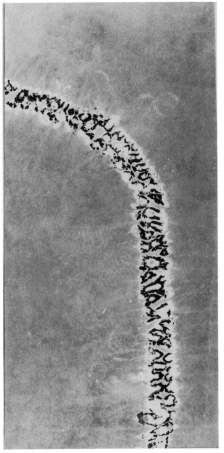

A series of stitches and folds carefully arranged can create a brick-like effect—*left*. Pat Obye *(detail)*

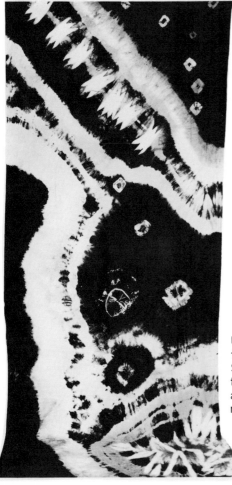

UNTITLED SILK PANEL. Multifarious and Quinja Maya. Silk. Some tie-dyes combine so many techniques they are difficult to analyze. In reality, the technique is not as important as the result.

TRITIK. Grace Earl. Discharge dye from navy blue fabric. A variety of stitches in various directions and shapes are combined in this presentation. One set of running and whipping stitches still in the fabric is the same as those used to create the pattern on the right side of the material.

MR. T.N. Marian Clayden. Hanging on Belgian linen using tritik. 72 inches high, 50 inches wide.

Courtesy, artist

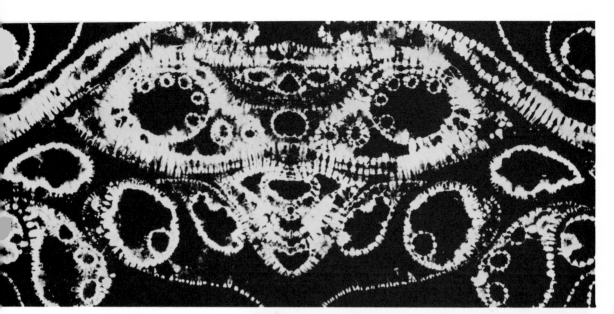

COMPOSITION WITH DYE AND THREAD. Hallie Redman. 24 inches high, 60 inches wide. A symmetrical, controlled design created by sewing a doubled fabric in various directions. Some shapes are made by tying in objects.

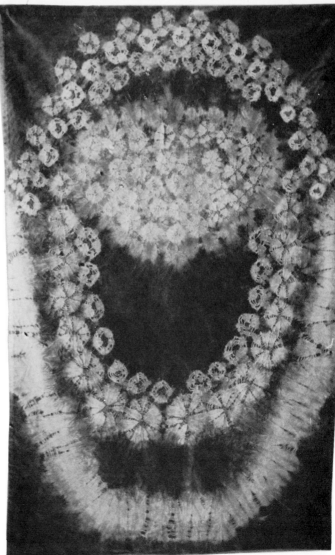

RADIANCE. Bernice Colman. Tie-dye velvet with gathered and stitched border. 50 inches high, 31 inches wide.
Courtesy, artist

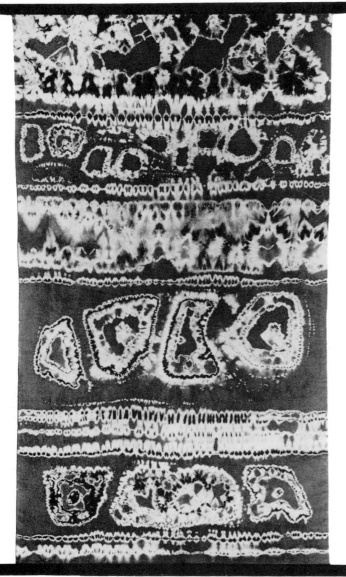

PEBBLES. June Mayborn Bonner. Dark blue cotton fabric, stitched and tied, then bleached. 34 inches high, 20 inches wide.

Courtesy, artist

WALL HANGING. Estelle Carlson. Tie-dye on muslin using several techniques. Dyeing and some bleaching. 108 inches high, 36 inches wide.

Courtesy, artist

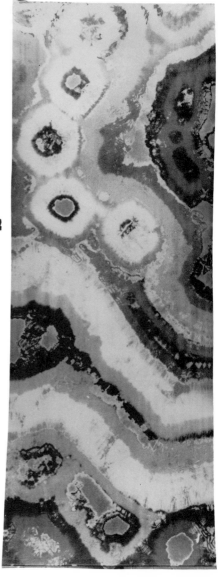

Pillows made in a variety of fabrics using many of the techniques described throughout this chapter. Will and Eileen Richardson.

CEREMONIAL ENCLOSURE.   Marian Clayden. Silk tie-dye in three related panels. 7½ feet high. Specially designed curved moldings support the fabric at top.

Photo, Lars Speyer

12

IDEAS FOR TIE-DYE PRESENTATION

THE potential of tie-dyed fabrics is unlimited and only beginning to be explored. Artists are combining any and all methods to achieve a greater dimension than the design created by the technique alone. They are to be commended for their imagination, ingenuity, and ability to fashion the fabrics into exciting artistic presentations.

Stitchery and quilting appear to be a natural combination with tie-dyed fabrics. After untying, the materials often remain raised because of the distortion of the fibers. Beth Ford and Lois Brooks have selected tied areas and brilliantly accented the relief design using needle and thread.

Phyllis Dukes has developed the idea of quilting tie-dye into three-dimensional soft sculptures. With the trend toward soft sculpture increasing, the bold, abstract shapes and wild colors obtained by tie-dyeing can inspire a new area for exploration.

Environments of tie-dye are already on the scene. Marion Clayden is rapidly moving from the single plane into floor-to-ceiling flat and undulating multiple panels that appear to reach out and invite you in. Multifarious and Quinja Maya have created an entire room: floor, walls, ceiling, furnishings, and wardrobe in their *Daytime Garden* (between pages 184 and 185). They are already envisioning another tie-dyeing environment to be called *The Nighttime Garden*.

Panels combined as framed diptychs and triptychs are used to expand the idea of a limited width of fabric. Someone is bound to carry the idea into polyptychs which we can surround and, perhaps eventually, surround us in an environmental fashion.

Tie-dye with batik is emerging as the synthesis of these two methods which are now being explored and exploited. Carolyn Roth McDade combines tie-dye, batik, and direct painting on canvas; sometimes the canvases are cut apart and reassembled.

It should be evident that there are no rules to follow, no one best way to create the designs you envision and to use the fabrics you design. The search for new uses and ideas for presentation is continual. It is a challenge to the artistic and expressive mentality of everyone who is stimulated by the statements still to be made with fabrics and dyes.

TIE-DYE MANDALA. Michi Ouchi. 88 inches high, 60 inches wide. White, pink, blue, and gray. A design can be carefully controlled and symmetrical by folding and dyeing.

Courtesy, artist

UNTITLED SILK PANEL.   Marian Clayden. 42 inches high, 42 inches wide. A design can be wildly abstract using tying and sewing techniques.

Photo, Lars Speyer

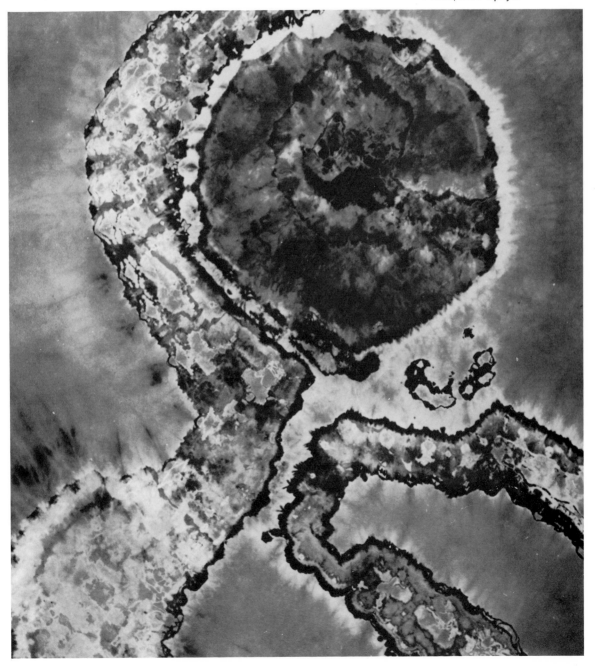

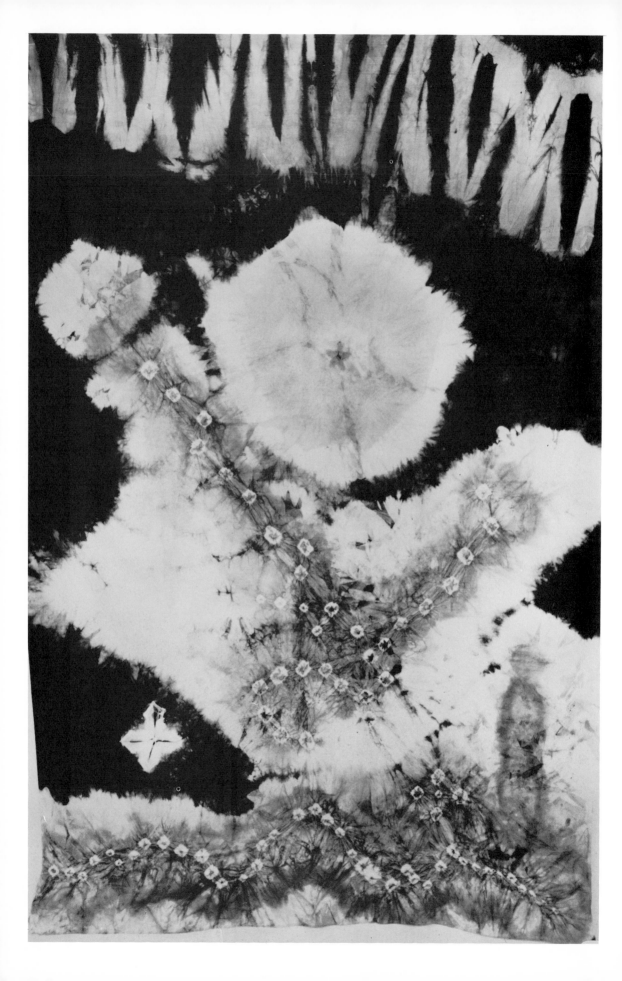

PATCHWORK BANNER. Julie Rheem Zaremba. Tie-dyed fabrics on cotton, corduroy, linen, and other materials were cut up and machine sewed onto a piece of black cotton backing in a patchwork design. The black backing was lined. 85 inches high, 50 inches wide.

DESIGN IN PURPLES. Estelle Carlson. Tie-dye with stitchery on linen and rayon. 54 inches high, 23 inches wide. To achieve a range of subtle colors Mrs. Carlson dyed some of the cords before using, then allowed the colors from the cords to bleed into the fabric on subsequent dippings. Some bleaching and redyeing were used.

Courtesy, artist

◄

UNTITLED. Multifarious and Quinja Maya. 3 yards. Cotton velveteen. Small tied areas create pattern and texture within the boldly designed areas of brilliant colors.

DISTANT PLACES.   Lois Brooks. Silk triptych. 8 feet high, 9 feet wide. Three panels were dyed separately but the design was planned to match exactly and create a larger design area. The idea was to expand the limiting design factor of "a width of material."

Courtesy, artist

MANDALA BANNER. Rita L. Shumaker. Tie-dye orange and red on white cotton with stuffed and quilted panel. Macramé fringe. 91 inches high, 45 inches wide.

Photo, Phil Drake

LATIN MEMORY. Lois Brooks. Tie-dye and quilting on silk. 60 inches high, 30 inches wide. First the piece was tie-dyed and then hand quilted on a frame using matching silk thread. The quilting responds to the individual quirks of the design and emphasizes the existing three-dimensional qualities of the tie-dyed area.

LATIN MEMORY (*detail*). Lois Brooks.
Photos, courtesy artist

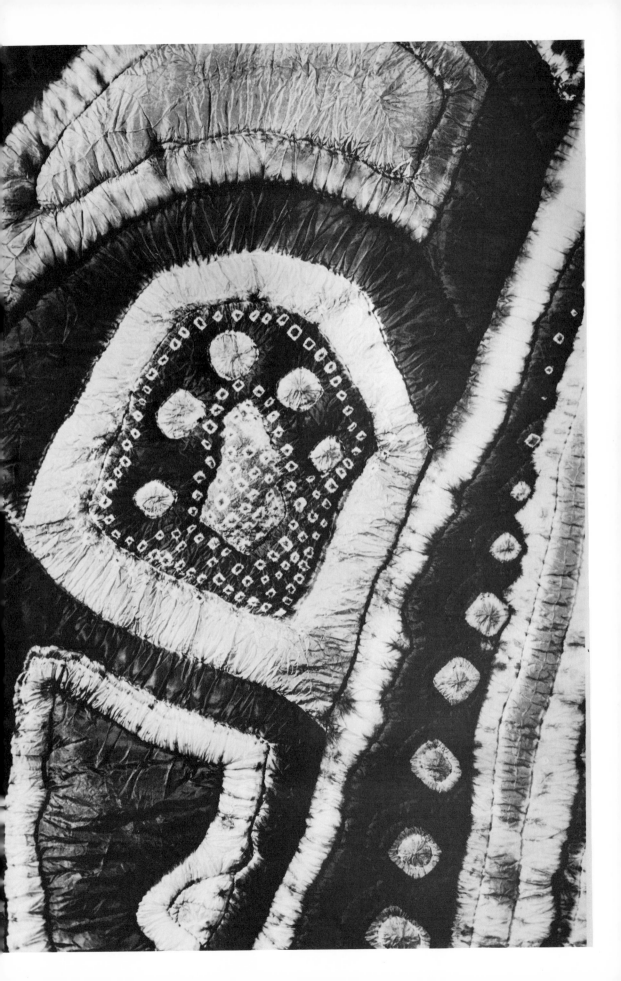

SUN BOWL. Phyllis Dukes. Machine stitched, quilted three-dimensional tie-dye. Colors, white, yellow, green, pink, and red.

Courtesy, artist

RECLUSE. Phyllis Dukes. Stuffed soft sculpture with appliqué and stitchery, using tie-dye fabric. 11 inches high, 10 inches wide, 7 inches deep. Colors, rust, red, and navy blue.

Courtesy, artist

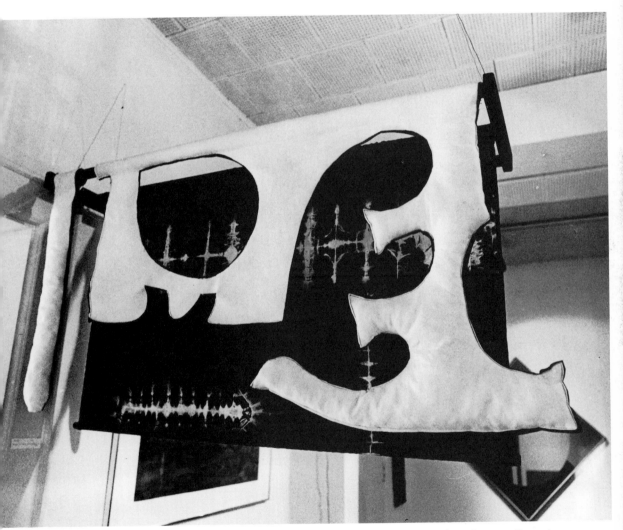

STELLAR. Rita L. Shumaker. Fold and dye discharge on black cotton; three layer unit used as a room divider. 25 inches high, 46 inches wide, 9 inches deep. The center panel is tie dyed. Stuffed, shaped felt constructions are hung on each side. On one side the felt is white on the outside, black on the inside; the other panel is reversed with black outside and white beneath.

Photo, Phil Drake

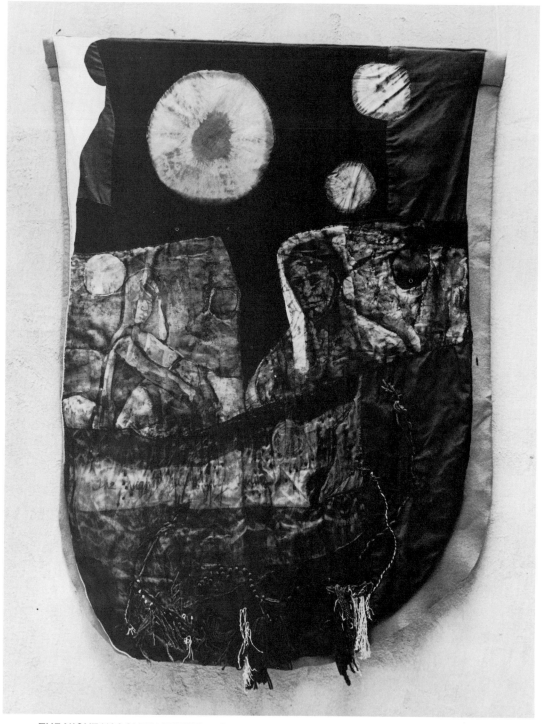

THE NIGHT HAS MANY MOONS.   Beth Ford. Batik and tie-dye with appliqué and stitchery. 7 feet high, 5 feet wide. White, hot pink, deep purple, and navy. Batik and tie-dye
areas of organdy are appliquéd and give transparent subtle color variations to the under
fabric. The large "moon" disc at top is padded with foam rubber.

Photo, Judy Durick

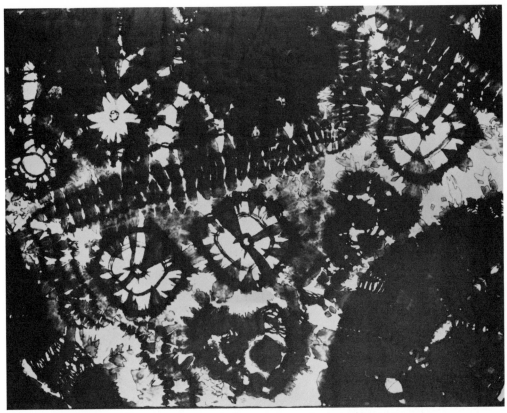

TIE DYE.   Pat Obye. Tie-dye designs are accentuated with quilting and hand stitching.

Detail of above.

FABRIC LENGTH. Gloria Perrino. Batik and tie-dye. 2½ yards. White areas were tied off and then the fabric was dipped in gold. After waxing over the white and gold, fabric was dipped in dark brown.

Courtesy, artist

THE MAGIC GARDEN. Stephen Blumrich. Tie-dye with batik on unbleached cotton muslin. 60 inches square. Twenty-one dye baths were used. Tie-dyed portions were used in the tree and tails of the birds. Some were untied and waxed during later dyebaths.

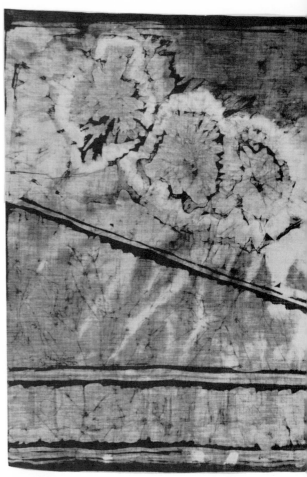

UNTITLED. Dona Meilach. Tie-dye discharge with batik. Green fabric tied with wire was dipped in bleach. The wire and bleach combination resulted in an oxidized coloration around the tied portions. Areas of the tie-dye and other sections were waxed and the fabric dipped in royal blue. It was further waxed and dipped in black for final crackle.

THERE SHE STOOD ON THE EDGE OF HER FEATHER, EXPECTING TO FLY. Carolyn Roth McDade. Tie-dye, batik, and acrylic painting on canvas in yellows and greens. 73 inches high, 61 inches wide. The canvas was first tie-dyed and then the large figure batiked. The small animal at bottom and the environmental elements were painted with acrylic.

Courtesy, artist

A length of fabric shaped into a tube makes an interesting floor to ceiling circular hanging. It is stitched to a wood ring at the top and bottom. A light can be placed within.

Classroom of Sister Mary Remy Revor, Mount Mary College, Milwaukee, Wis.

◄

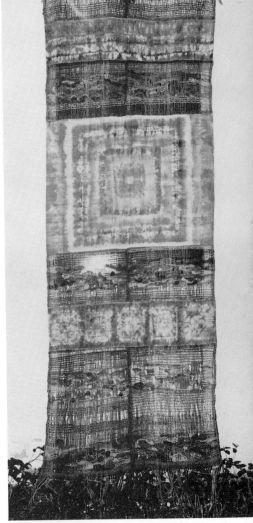

►

IKAT WEAVING WITH TIE-DYE PANEL. Karen Chang. Tie-dyed silk warps. 90 inches high, 40 inches wide.

Courtesy, artist

TIE-DYE PANEL.   Judith Irany. A panel of fabric can double as a wall hanging or a table cover.

SNAKE IN THE GRASS. Carolyn Roth McDade. Tie-dye and acrylic painting. 60 inches high, 80 inches wide. The entire canvas was first tie-dyed then cut into three sections. Upper section was dyed blue, the bottom section was batiked (the form of the snake) and dyed blue. The sections were resewn, the canvas stretched and the flowers and landscapes added with acrylics.

Collection, I.B.M. Building,
Chattanooga, Tenn.

SOFT SCULPTURE (detail). Karen Chang. Tie-dyed silks and velveteens have a rich, shimmering quality when stuffed into vegetable shapes and combined with crochet.

Courtesy, artist

GARDEN FORMS. Lois Brooks. Tie-dye and batik. 9 feet high, 3 feet wide. Turquoise dye was applied by brushing on. The fabric was tie-dyed with orange, creating extraordinary patterns where the turquoise bled out of the painted dye. The dark blue and purple lines were added last by the batik method.

Courtesy, artist

DRESS.   Rita Shumaker. Tie-dye using the discharge technique on black cotton. Slit sleeves are lined with white crepe.

Photo, John Daughtry

13

TIE-DYE AND BATIK CLOTHING AND OTHER ACCESSORIES

IT IS fun to make utilitarian items from dyed fabrics and in the following pages you'll find several examples that can send you to your cutting board and sewing machine. For many years the tie-dye technique has been associated with teenage efforts at decorating T-shirts and blue jeans. But high fashion designers have observed the varieties of design possible in the methods and yards of the fabrics have been especially created for haute couture.

With this impetus, many artist-craftsmen recognize the efficacy of using their individually created fabrics for fashioning unique clothes for themselves and for sale through craft shops around the country. None are in the mass production business so such clothes must be sought from the creator or the crafts shop. For those who are not handy with a needle, and who wish to use the fabrics for clothes, it is wise to team up with a dressmaker. One craftsman suggests swapping services; making two pieces of fabric length and trading the seamstress one of them for her services. Some dress designers seek the craftsmen who will create special fabrics for individual fashions.

Fabrics for clothes may be conceived in two ways; the fabric may be dyed first and then the clothing parts cut from it; or the pattern may be pre-conceived, the pieces cut and then the design dyed on the cut pieces. That way you can plan a pattern for a dress front and back, up one sleeve or around a neckline.

All dyes for clothing fabrics should be carefully selected and suggested washing or dry cleaning methods followed.

For best dyeing results, use the natural fibers recommended earlier: cottons, silks, linens, and wool. Remember that permanent-press fabrics should be pre-treated to remove the finish. Select dyes that are high in light- and washfastness or that will withstand several dry cleanings. Leathers and suedes can be batiked and tie-dyed for clothing, using fiber reactive dyes or the aniline dyes sold for coloring leather. Always experiment on scraps to find the ability of a specific hide to absorb color; tanning methods and coloring will affect the absorption of additional dyes. Ask for garment leather when you make your purchases.

HOODED CAFTAN. Rita Shumaker.
Fold-and-dye discharge on brown velveteen resulted in brown and gold
colors.

Photo, John Daughtry

DRESS. Rita Shumaker. Tie-dye and
fold-dye dress of cotton broadcloth.
Four colors on white cotton: blue, red,
and rust produced some overdyes of
pinks.

Photo, John Daughtry

LONG WRAP. Pat Nichelson. Fold-dye on cotton.

Courtesy, artist

CASUAL DRESS. Pat Nichelson. Fold-dye on cotton.

Courtesy, artist

DRESS. Rita Shumaker. Tie-dye and fold-dye dress of cotton broadcloth lined with deep blue taffeta. Dress is light blue, jade green, and deep blue.

Photo, John Daughtry

PANT SKIRT. Susan J. Larson. Fold-and-tie discharge on dark blue fabric resulted in tones of lighter blue-gray.

SUNDRESS. Rita Shumaker. Ties and folds overdyed on lavender duck cloth. Colors are lavender, wine, and brown.

Photo, John Daughtry

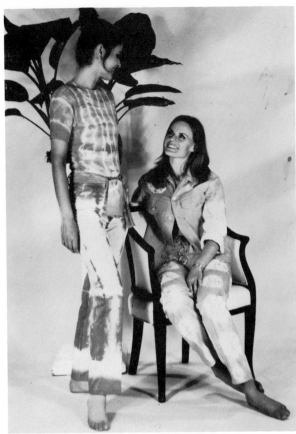

Casual clothes. *(Left)* Blouse and jeans fold-dyed. *(Right)* Pants with matching skirt tie-dyed.

Courtesy, Dylon International Unlimited

Shawl and long culottes. Beth Ford. Tie-dye on muslin with fringe and leather thongs. Colors, white, yellow, green, rust, and black.

Photo, Judy Durick

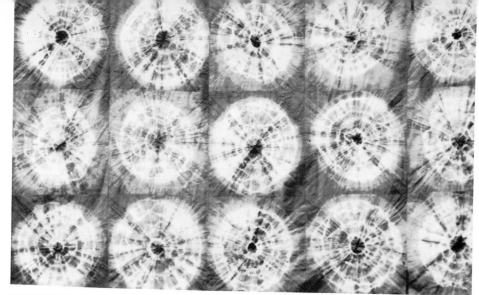

BEDSPREAD (*detail*). Joy Lobell. Individually tie-dyed squares were sewed together to make a bedspread. The same technique could be used for different sizes and shapes of fabrics. Small and individually tied or fold-dyed pieces can be assembled in a random or orderly arrangement and fashioned into a variety of garments or accessories.

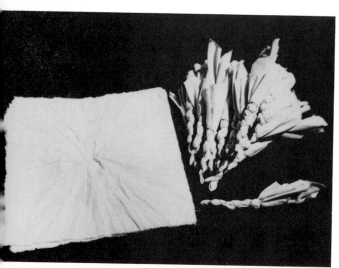

The 16-inch squares of white muslin are individually wrapped with rubber bands and dyed light brown in the washing machine. Edges should be torn, rather than cut, so they will be straighter.

They were unwrapped and retied in the same way but in different places and redyed in dark brown. The squares were sewed together to make the bedspread. Mrs. Lobell felt it was easier to tie and dye smaller pieces evenly than to tie an entire piece of fabric at one time. If one square did not dye quite right, the whole piece would not be a disaster.

Scarves tie- and fold-dyed in different arrangements are attractive, colorful, and practical.
Courtesy, Dylon International Unlimited

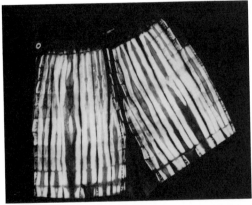

SHORTS. Pat Obye. Fold-dyed. An additional color was achieved by holding the folds with metal bulldog clips so the reaction of the dye chemicals and salt with the metal oxidized and resulted in a rust color along the fold line.

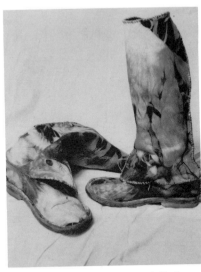

LEATHER BOOTS. Multifarious and Quinja Maya. Shoe boots tie-dyed.

LEATHER KNAPSACK. Multifarious and Quinja Maya. Tie-dyed very soft leather is sewn into a shoulder sack.

DRESS. Beth Ford. Batik on cotton. Dress parts were precut and then batiked so designs would match. Colors, white with beige and navy blue.

Photo, Judy Durick

MAN'S SHIRT. Marian L. Martin. Batik shirt on 100 percent white cotton. First pattern was of yellow coin dots and diamonds. The second dyeing was brown and then crackled in black for final dye.

TIES. Susan J. Larson. Tie-dyed and fold-dyed fabrics made into men's ties.
Photo, Jim Zinn

BATIK TIES. Lifcha Alper. Cotton and linen ties are lined with silk.

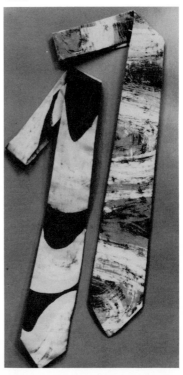

PAINTED MASK (*shirt*). Dolores Ashley-Harris. White, peach, wine, and brown on cotton.

Photo, Joe Zinn

14

DYES AND HOW TO
USE THEM

WHEN people who do batik and tie-dye meet, their first question usually is, "What kind of dyes do you use?" The quest for relatively easy to use, permanent, colorfast dyes is never ending. Modern textile chemistry has come a long way but it still hasn't solved all these problems relative to all fabrics. Even industrially dyed materials fade in time. So the home dyer must use what is available and constantly search for new developments in dye chemistry.

At first, the dye vocabulary, assistants, and methods may seem formidable, but with a little experience, you'll be stirring up batches of dye as readily as you put together a meat loaf or cake. Mixing dye formulas is much like mixing recipes and after you are familiar with the components, what they do, and how you can follow and vary the formulas, you'll soon be a pro.

One misconception to be cleared up surrounds the word "aniline" which often is erroneously used to describe a specific dye. The word aniline, in common usage, refers to synthetic dyes. Its application to dyeing evolved in 1856 when the English chemist Sir Henry Perkins accidentally produced aniline purple while trying to make quinine from aniline. Aniline, a colorless, oily liquid, has become one of the most valuable chemicals used in making dyes, inks, varnishes, and other colorants.

Until 1856, and Perkins's discovery, dyes were made either from natural materials such as butternut, hickory, roots, and berries; or from minerals such as rocks and mud. Today synthetic dyes are used almost exclusively. They are derived from coal tar substances and composed of aniline along with various other chemicals.

Synthetic dyes used for fabrics are divided into different classes depending upon their use and their composition. To determine the class of dye to use, you must know the fabric to be dyed. With only natural fibers used in batik and tie-dye, cotton and linen, silk and wool, this simplifies matters. The chart on page 266 will quickly show which class of dye to use with which fabrics.

One can become easily confused by dye brand names: many distributors delight in packaging products so the contents are kept a mystery. Actually, there are only about four manufacturers of all dyestuffs; every distributor must buy from these manufacturers. This means that the dyes you buy packaged under one label with one set of directions could be essentially the same dyestuff you can buy under other labels with slight variations in the formula.

The chart on page 266 will help you decide, by brand name, the class of a specific dyestuff. For example, fiber-reactive dyes are manufactured by ICI America, Inc., under their trade name Procion and are distributed by several companies. Comparing the directions from all distributors reveals that they are essentially the same with only slight differences in procedures; some provide a fixing agent with their own label, but it must always be washing soda (sal soda) no matter what they call it. It follows, therefore, that the formula given by one distributor for a specific class of dye can be used with the same class of dye sold by any other distributor.

HOW DYES WORK

To visualize how dyes work, think of them as molecules penetrating the fibers of the fabric. This is different from the action of a *pigment* such as acrylic paints, oil paints, and printing inks which lie on top of, or coat, the fabric rather than penetrating it. The drawing, below, visually illustrates how the different dye classes enter the fibers.

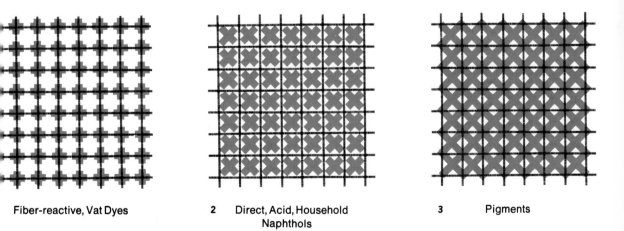

Fiber-reactive, Vat Dyes   2   Direct, Acid, Household
                                      Naphthols
                                                              3   Pigments

The dotted lines represent the fibers of the fabrics; the +'s represent the dye molecules. 1) Fiber reactive and vat dyes actually become part of the fiber itself and exhibit exceptional washfastness. 2) In direct, acid, and household dyes, the black +'s, which represent the dye, penetrate their way in between the fiber pores and sort of hibernate in the fiber after fixing with a salt compound. They exhibit poor washfastness because of their ability to be pulled off the fiber. 3) Pigments overlap or actually coat the fiber. They are not very washfast unless they are bonded to the fiber with a resin compound.

FUNCTION OF ASSISTANTS—SALT AND ACETIC ACID

All dyes require an assistant, either salt or acetic acid (depending upon the fiber to be dyed). In most formulas you add the assistant to the dyebath. In some household dyes, salt is already mixed in. The purpose of the assistant is to help the dye combine with the fiber. Salt must be present in a dye formula for dying cotton and linen. It is an electrolyte and helps drive the dye molecules into the fiber. Without salt the dye will only stain the fabric and be easily rinsed out. Common (uniodized) salt is available from the grocery store.

Acetic acid is used in formulas for dying silk and wool. It can be purchased from the drugstore, a chemical supply source, or a photo shop as glacial acetic acid. White vinegar from the grocery store is a dilute 5 percent acetic acid. See acid dyes for formulas.

When a dye calls for alcohol to paste the dye, use wood alcohol from a paint store and not rubbing alcohol.

FRESHNESS OF MIXTURES

A dye formula is most active when it is freshly mixed. The color intensity depends on the molecules in the solution. As the fabric absorbs the color, fewer dye molecules remain in the dyebath. Therefore, when you dye several pieces of fabric in one dyebath, those that are dyed first will have the strongest color.

By the time the last piece of fabric is placed in the dye, most of the molecules will have been used. The longer the fabric is in the dye, the more molecules will enter the fabric. It is not unusual to observe that very little color remains in the dyebath after the fabric has been in it for some time.

HOT AND COLD DYEING

The majority of dyes are made for hot dyeing at simmering temperatures of about 140°. Under these heat conditions the dye molecules exhaust themselves into the fabric most efficiently and result in the optimum color brilliance and fastness. These are excellent for tie-dye. For batik high temperature dyes cannot be used because the wax would melt. When hot dyes are used at cool temperatures, they should be kept at as high a temperature as possible so as not to melt the wax and yet be efficient. An average temperature of 90° to 100° is usually safe. The colder the solution, the less effective the dye.

The best dyes for batik, therefore, are those that can be used cold. The only class of dyes made specifically for cold dyeing are fiber reactive and even they are recommended for a 100° dyebath. Their light- and washfastness are excellent and the colors are brilliant. Fiber reactive dyes attach to the fiber differently from other dyes: they actually link and form a bond with the fiber molecules, thereby increasing their permanence.

Other classes of dyes most commonly used for batik and tie-dye are:

DIRECT DYES

Mainly for cotton, linen, and viscose rayon. Common salt is the assistant. They are most efficient when used hot but can be cooled down for batik.

ACID DYES

For silk and wool. Acetic acid is the assistant. They too are most efficient at hot temperatures but adaptable to cool dyeing.

ALL-PURPOSE HOUSEHOLD DYES (*union dyes*)

For all fabrics including synthetics. The assistant depends upon the material being dyed. A package of household dye usually consists of a mix of direct, acid, and other dyes for synthetics. Only the molecules of dye absorbed by the materials being dyed are used; the others are sloughed off. Good for blends of fabrics. Most efficient for hot dyeing; must be used cooled for batik.

VAT DYES AND NAPHTHOL DYES are special classes that are more fully described beginning on page 261.

GENERAL PROCEDURES FOR DYEING

Before you begin, gather all the items you will need. Use dyeing vessels of enamel, plastic, or glass and large enough to accommodate the fabric without crowding. Laundry tubs, old washing machines, and bathtubs can be used. Mixing and measuring utensils should also be glass, plastic, or stainless steel. Small glass jars are handy for pasting and dissolving the dyestuffs.

Wear rubber gloves (some dyes dissolve plastic gloves) and an apron. If you plan to store stock solutions, have jars ready. Soft water, preferred for dyeing, can be obtained by adding ¼ teaspoon Calgon water softener per pint of dye. To aid in level dyeing (even dye penetration), it is sometimes necessary to add about 1 teaspoon of mild liquid detergent or soap to the dyebath. This varies from dye to dye and from fabric to fabric and can only be determined by experimenting.

MIXING THE DYESTUFF

Generally, follow package instructions. Some packaging, however, lacks adequate instructions. Then, compare any given facts on the package against the chart on page 266, determine the dye classification, and proceed according to the instructions for that class of dye.

Dyes usually are "pasted" or mixed with a few tablespoons of cold water, then dissolved in a cup of hot water. If lumps remain, strain the dye through a couple of layers of fine cloth. Then add the dye to the dyebath. Dissolve and add the assistant. Only after all powders are dissolved should you add the fabric.

AMOUNTS OF DYESTUFF TO USE: DIRECT, ACID, HOUSEHOLD

The amount of dyestuff to use depends on the color intensity you want. At first, you will tend to use more dyestuff than necessary trying to determine color intensity by how it looks in the water. This is not always valid. Color can be made more dilute or more intense by the amount of water in the bath. But the most reliable system is to base color intensity on the proportion of dyestuff to the weight of the fabric. For the most accurate, and economical, use of *direct, acid,* and *household* dyes the following general measures apply:

For 1 pound of fabric: (about 3 yards, 36-inch width, medium weight)
  ½ to 1½ teaspoons dyestuff to 1 pound fabric for pale intensity
  1½ to 4 teaspoons dyestuff to 1 pound fabric for medium intensity
  4 to 6 teaspoons dyestuff to 1 pound fabric for deep intensity

You must also measure the assistants based on the fabric weight
  For salt, figure 3 tablespoons for 1 pound of fabric
  For acetic acid, figure 4 teaspoons for 1 pound of fabric

The amount of water must always cover the fabric . . . but roughly figure:
  2½ gallons of water for 1 pound of fabric

Adding too much water will weaken the color. Too little water will give a darker color in the same time period. Increasing the water temperature will hasten the dye process and lowering the temperature will slow it down. The length of time the dye is in the dyebath will also affect intensity.

Therefore, to duplicate colors, you should record all factors. Summarized, these include:

  1. Weight of the fabric
  2. Amount of dyestuff
  3. Amount of salt or acetic acid
  4. Amount of water
  5. Amount of agitation
  6. Temperature of water
  7. Length of dyeing time

After the dyebath is prepared, use a strip of fabric to test intensity remembering that colors appear darker when wet. If the color is too pale, add more pasted and dissolved dye. Always remove the fabric before adding dye so as not to spot the cloth unevenly. Figure dyeing time beginning with the last addition of color.

It is possible to use dyes from different classes on one fabric providing they are for the same fiber content. For instance, you can use fiber reactive dyes and then overdye with direct dyes on cotton or linen. Of course, colorfastness properties will be altered and one should experiment.

WETTING OUT: DYEING: RINSING

The batik or dyed fabric should be wet out before placing it in the dyebath to insure a thorough and even dye saturation. Soak the fabric in lukewarm or cool water (if the fabric is waxed) for 3 to 5 mintues. Remove, let the

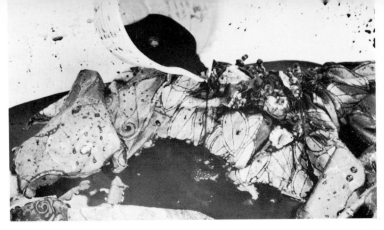

Instead of stirring fabric and over-cracking the wax, you can keep the dye moving by pouring it over the fabric with a cup.

water drip off, then immerse the fabric in the dyebath. Stir or agitate the material as recommended for the specific dye. To avoid excess crackle in batik, keep the solution moving by using a cup to pour dye over the material. Leave fabric in dyebath recommended amount of time, adding additional assistants or fixers required for specific classes of dyes.

Remove fabric from dye and place in a rinse bath using lukewarm water and rinse until the water runs clear. Lay fabrics out to dry on wax paper or plastic. Hanging them on a line can cause the color to migrate so the bottom of the fabric will become darker than the top. Fiber clotheslines may also absorb some of the dye and create a streak across the fabric. Fiber reactive dyes should be dried slowly and thoroughly. Other dye instructions may suggest ironing the fabric while still damp to help set the color.

FIXING THE COLOR

Color is fixed by heat (except fiber reactives) and usually ironing a tie-dyed fabric with a steam iron is sufficient. For batik the heat generated in ironing out the wax helps set the dye. Individual classes of dyes require different fixing methods and directions for fixing and finishing should be followed.

STORING DYES

Dye powders usually do not deteriorate as long as they are not mixed. Once mixed with water, a stock solution can be stored for a few days to a few weeks. After the assistant, salt or vinegar, has been mixed with the dyebath, the solution cannot be stored because the color properties exhaust rapidly. That is why freshly mixed dyes are recommended for optimum results. You can experiment, of course. Many dyes can be used within 24 hours after mixing and still color a piece of fabric adequately. Use a test strip to determine strength of dyes. Some dyes will store longer if refrigerated and such questions can be directed to the distributor or answered by trial and error.

Often, stored mixed dyes will form an algae and they should be discarded. Dye particles precipitate out of solution and will not remix. However, school-teachers constantly store and reuse dyes and refute the advice of many chemists.

Store dyes in quart, one-half gallon, and gallon glass or plastic bottles which may be purchased for the purpose. It is more economical to secure used salad and juice jars from restaurants and drive-ins which normally discard them. Plastic bottles used for photography chemicals are readily available.

CLASSES OF DYES, GENERAL CHARACTERISTICS AND FORMULAS

There are various classes of dyes and many brands within a class. Veteran textile artists often admit that dye chemistry is confusing so they find one type of dye and stick with it. Yet the chemistry can be easily sorted out and the discussion of each class of dye, the photos, and general formula for mixing should simplify identifying them and using them. Colorfastness of individual colors within a classification differs. A standard reference for light- and wash-fastness of each class of dye can be found in *The Color Index,* a set of resource volumes published by the American Association of Textile Chemists and Colorists.* The volumes are available in libraries in most large cities, and in colleges and universities with strong chemistry departments. First check the class of dyes such as fiber reactive, direct, and so forth, then the individual color which is rated on a scale of 1 to 7 for light- and washfastness.

Dyes discussed and illustrated are those used by artists whose work appears in this book. They are available from craft shops or from mail order supply sources listed in the appendix. Other dye distributors have the same classes of dyes under their own labels. Many industrial distributors will charge for packaging when only a few pounds of a color are ordered. Schools, and artists ordering together, can benefit from bulk buying. For specific distributors other than those listed, consult the *Dye* listing in your classified telephone book or the *Thomas Register* available in the library. Write for a member list from the American Association of Textile Chemists, Research Triangle Park, North Carolina 27709.

FIBER REACTIVE DYES

Fiber reactive dyes are made principally by ICI America, Inc., under their trade name of Procion M Series for cold water dyeing. Procion dyes were discovered in England in 1956 and are called fiber reactive because the dye

* In England, it is published by The Society of Dyers and Colorists, Bradford, Yorkshire.

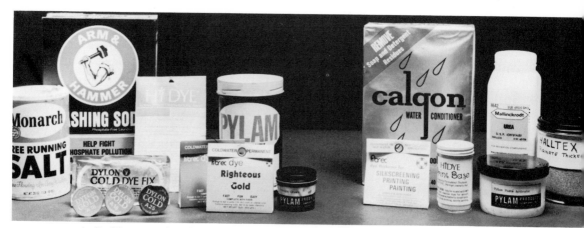

Left. Fiber reactive dyes are distributed by several companies. They require salt and washing soda. *Right.* They are thickened for direct application with Calgon, urea, and sodium alginate, or with prepared thickening mixtures (see chapter 6).

molecule forms a bond with the fiber and, therefore, is permanent and fast to light and washing.

Several distributors are packaging Procion dyes in small quantities for the craftsman under such names as Dylon, Fabdec, Fibrec, Hi Dye, Pylam, and Putnam. The original formula presented several years ago has been simplified and the length of dyeing time reduced so that fiber reactive dyes are now among the most popular used for batik. They are most efficient in 90° to 100° dyebaths that will not melt the wax.

Directions for using fiber reactive dyes differ by distributors and many market their own fixing agents but so long as you know a dye is fiber reactive, you can use any set of directions. You can determine its class by checking any known facts about the fixer or dye procedure against the chart on page 268. Fiber reactive dyes require salt for the assistant and washing soda (sal soda) as the fixer. They may be thickened for direct application following the formula in chapter 6, page 112.

There are two methods for dyeing: a short, 30-minute method and a longer, 2-hour method. The short method is suggested for small quantities of fabric. The longer method is recommended for larger pieces of fabric. Either method, however, will give satisfactory results for small or large pieces.

The following can be used to determine the intensity of the shade for 1 pound of cloth which, for medium weight fabrics, is about 3 yards, 36-inch width:

| | DYESTUFF | | SALT | |
Shade	Grams	Teaspoons	Grains	Tablespoons
Pale	.75	¼	90	3
Medium	1.50	½	180	6
Heavy	3.00	1 to 3	240	9 to 15

SHORT DYEING METHOD

1. Paste dye in cold water and then dissolve in about 1 cup hot water 140° and mix in dyebath of 90° to 100°.
2. Add common salt to dyebath.
3. Place fabric in dyebath for 10 minutes turning the fabric constantly or pouring the dye over the fabric with a cup to avoid crackling the wax.
4. Dissolve 2 level tablespoons washing soda (sal soda) or specific fixer in 2 tablespoons warm water. Remove fabric, add soda to dye, stir, and replace fabric.
5. Dye for 15 minutes stirring occasionally.
6. Remove fabric and rinse under cool water. Lay out to dry on non-absorbent paper or place in plastic clothes bag for two hours and then dry. Fiber reactive dyes continue to set as they dry so *never* dry rapidly.
7. Finishing. Rinse in cool water, then warm water to remove any excess dye, then wash with hot water and detergent in a washing machine.

For batik: The soda sometimes eats into the wax so rewaxing areas may be necessary when several dippings are planned. After drying fabric, iron out wax, then finish. (*Note:* some people prefer to rinse only after all dyebaths are completed.)

For tie-dye: Rinse fabric and dry thoroughly before untying. Dye colors continue to set as they dry so if fabrics are untied too soon, the colors are apt to slip under the ties. They also tend to dye the ties themselves so tie-dye with fiber reactives is a little tricky and should be tested.

LONG DYE METHOD

A non-automatic washing machine can be used for the dyeing described below so you don't have to stand over the fabric and stir for such long periods. An old bathtub or child's swimming pool or other apparatus rigged up on automobile seat springs can also be improvised. These directions are also based on 1 pound of fabric.

1. Mix dye and add to dyebath as above. Add fabric and stir for 10 minutes.
2. Then add salt to the dyeing in 3 equal parts with 5 minutes between additions, using the amounts given above for the shade desired. Stir between salt additions. Continue stirring for 20 minutes after all the salt is in.
3. Dissolve 3 tablespoons washing soda per pound of fabric in a small amount of warm water and add to the dyeing. Dye for 1 hour more, stirring continuously for the first 10 minutes and every 5 minutes or so for the rest of the time.
4. Rinse cloth, dry, and finish as in steps 6 and 7 short method.

Note: Turquoise cannot be dyed successfully by cold water immersing and, therefore, cannot be used for batik. For those who want to use turquoise for tie-dye, use the following procedure. After the addition of salt, heat the dye with fabric immersed to 180° to 190° and simmer. Then add 9 to 12 tablespoons of dissolved washing soda and stir for 5 minutes. Continue to simmer for about 15 minutes stirring frequently. Rinse and follow general procedures for finishing.

Procion black is not recommended for dip dyeing. To get a close black, mix 6 parts navy blue, 3 parts scarlet, 3 parts yellow, and use 4 to 5 times the amount of dyestuff as for lighter colors.

FOR DYEING WOOL WITH FIBER REACTIVES

Dyeing wool requires heat so wool may be used for tie-dye but not for batik. Mix dye and all of salt as for the short-method dipping. Place dyebath on stove with fabric and heat to simmer and maintain for about 10 minutes. Then add 1 cup white vinegar to dyebath or the proportion of ¼ cup vinegar to 1 gallon of water. Simmer for 10 minutes more. (Do not add washing soda or other fixer.) Remove from heat, rinse in hot water, then hand wash in hot soapy water and rerinse. Avoid sudden temperature changes in water; it can damage and shrink wool. Do not machine wash.

FIXING FIBER REACTIVE DYES

Fiber reactive dyes are fixed by the action of the washing soda which creates an alkaline solution needed to make the dye and fiber molecules react. No additional heat or moisture is required. Washing in hot soapy water is recommended to eliminate excess dye. However, many people still like to steam, bake, or iron the fabric, using the same procedures given for direct application, pages 114–115.

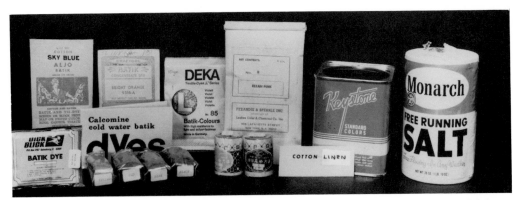

DIRECT DYES for cotton, linen, and viscose rayon are distributed by Aljo, Dick Blick, Craftool, Calcomine, Deka, Fezan, Keystone, 7K, and Miyako. They are most efficient at high temperatures but can be used in lukewarm 90° to 100° dyebaths for batik. When using them lukewarm it is a good practice to double the amount of dye used for hot dyeing. Salt is the assistant at a ratio of about 3 tablespoons per pound of fabric.

The general procedures include pasting and dissolving the dye, then adding it to the dyebath. Individual distributors vary the instructions for the amount of time the fabric is in the dyebath and whether to rinse the fabric before or after drying. Follow package instructions but do experiment. The intensity of color can be greatly controlled by the amount of time in the dyebath as well as by the amount of dyestuff used in relation to the weight of the fabric. For direct applications, use the same thickening formula given on page 112 for fiber reactive dyes but omit the sodas.

Light- and washfastness of direct dyes are rated poor to excellent so dry cleaning of dyed fabrics is recommended.

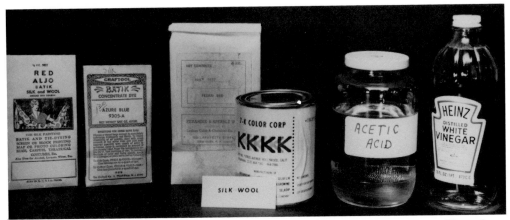

ACID DYES are so called because they are applied in an acid dyebath on silk and wool. This is accomplished by the addition of acetic acid as the assistant. Acetic acid is available from a chemical supply house, drugstore, or photography shop as glacial acetic acid. White vinegar from the grocery store is a dilute 5 percent acid. Some formulas use Glauber's salt, which is sodium sulfate, also available from a chemical supply house.

Convenient conversion:

2 tablespoons acetic acid = ½ cup white vinegar
Glacial acetic acid should be cut down to about 30 percent with water for use in dyebaths.

Follow general dye procedure for both cool and hot dye immersion methods for batik and tie-dye. Wool should be wet out, dyed, and rinsed at the same temperatures to avoid matting the fibers and to reduce shrinkage. Acid dyes are available from Aljo, Craftool, Fezan, Keystone, 7K, and Aiko.

Acid dyes generally produce bright clear shades. They are rated fair to poor in washing, good in dry cleaning and lightfastness.

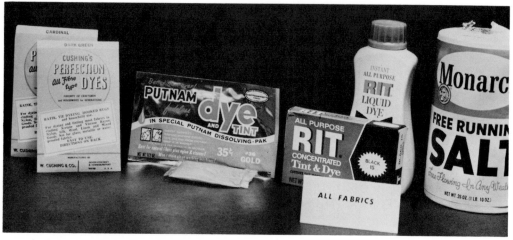

HOUSEHOLD DYES (union dyes) are considered all purpose. They contain a mixture of basic, acid, and other dyestuffs applicable to synthetics and will dye blends of fabrics. Colors are excellent in hot solutions, poor in cold dyeing. Brands such as Dylon Multipurpose, Cushing's, Putnam, Rit, and Tintex are readily available in drugstore, grocery stores, and dime stores. They can be used on cottons, silks, linens, wool, and many of the man-made fibers such as acetate, nylon, and some polyesters.

For hot dyeing follow package directions; for cold dyeing, see general directions for dyeing, page 112, and add double the amount of dye recommended for hot dyeing.

Household dyes are poor to good in lightfastness and washfastness. Dyed fabrics should not be washed with other fabrics as the colors tend to run even after several launderings. They can be dry cleaned.

Salt is the assistant and many dyes already have the salt added. For wool, some recipes call for vinegar. Dick Blick, an all-purpose dye sold for batiking, calls for pasting the dye in wood alcohol as the assistant, but salt should be used also.

Color is set by ironing the fabric while damp.

VAT DYES

Vat dyes are unique in that the colors develop after they are put on the fabric and exposed to light and heat. 1) When dye is applied you cannot tell what color it is. 2) Colors as they develop in the sun at three minutes. 3) at five minutes. 4) at ten minutes.

1

2

3

4

VAT DYES are for cotton, linen, silk, and viscose rayon. They have excellent fastness properties. Inkodye, specifically marketed for craftsmen, contains the necessary assistants. It can be used for dipping and direct dye application with a special thickener.

Vat dyes are actually pigments that must be changed into a leuco base by the addition of lye and caustic soda. In the leuco base state, dyes do not exhibit their final color, but they are able to combine with the fibers as a dye, not a pigment. When dry- and heat-treated, the colors develop and they are fixed as a pigment which combines *with* the fabric fiber rather than coating it as pigments normally do. Inkodye already has the additions in it so the use of lye and other chemicals is not required.

Dyes are developed by heat. The fabric must be exposed to warm, direct sunlight while it is damp, or it may be developed by ironing slowly with a household iron. It can also be baked in a 280° oven for 15 to 60 minutes. A flat piece of fabric will develop in 5 minutes when placed on a cookie sheet. A tie-dyed piece will take longer. To avoid the hazard of melting and fire, waxed fabrics should not be put in an oven. Dyed fabrics may also be placed in a steamer or pressure cooker for about 20 minutes. Fabrics must be set by dry-steaming to prevent the colors from running.

After the dyes are set, residual chemicals are removed by rinsing the fabric in warm water and washing in soapy water and rerinsing.

For dip-dyeing, the dye should be diluted to 1 part water for 1 part dye for vivid colors, up to 4 parts of water for pastels.

For printing and direct painting, the dye can be used as is or extended with Inkodye clear to produce lighter values. Direct painting in sunlight can be explored because the colors develop as you work.

NAPHTHOL DYES are generally not recommended by chemists or dye distributors for the home dyer. Naphthol dyes, also called azoic, are not packaged for craftsmen, and sources for the ingredients are not easy to find. Yet many craftsmen use and swear by Naphthol dyes for cottons and linens because they are extremely colorfast. They are the dyes used by the Javanese. Procedures differ with different artists. The following is offered by June Mayborn Bonner who has reduced the system to 2 baths. Dyes are called fast-color salts and have a normal shelf life of only about one year. The general procedure involves mixing 2 baths. The first bath uses Naphthol and Monopol Oil (sulfonated castor oil) mixed with caustic soda (sodium hydroxide) in proportions depending upon the color to be used.

For the second bath, water, Calgon, common salt, and fast-color salts are used. The wet fabric is put first in the Naphthol bath and then in the second bath with the color, then rinsed and dried.

You will need:

Rubber gloves
2 dye pots (plastic dishpan, pail, etc.)
2 small bowls
2 pint containers
1 empty plastic detergent bottle (1 quart) for caustic

caustic flakes (sodium hydroxide) from the chemist or you can also use drain cleaner from the grocery store
common salt
Calgon
Naphthol ⎫
Fast-color salts ⎬ from GAF or American Hoechst Corporation
Monopol Oil ⎭

A. Prepare caustic mix—use the 1 quart detergent bottle and mix 8 tablespoons dry caustic soda in one quart of cold water. This is a stock solution that will keep indefinitely.
B. Prepare Naphthol solution in pot number 1.

1. Use enough water to cover fabric and allow it to float freely. Use water at about 85°; add 1 tablespoon of Calgon to soften and 2 tablespoons common salt.
2. Paste 1 tablespoon of Naphthol with 1 tablespoon Monopol Oil in a small bowl. Add hot water until dissolved and put in one of the pint containers with another cup of hot water. To this add about ½ tablespoon caustic soda and mix all together. Pour this Naphthol solution into pot number 1.

C. Mix color in pot number 2.

1. Put the same amount of water into pot number 2 with the same amount of Calgon and salt as above.
2. Paste 1 tablespoon of fast-color salt with cool water; add more water and mix into second pint container with enough cool water to completely dissolve salt. This may take 5 to 10 minutes.
3. Pour color mixture from pint container into pot number 2.

To Dye

1. Wet the fabric in plain water.
2. Move fabric into pot number 1 (the Naphthol solution) and stir for 10 minutes.
3. Move fabric from pot 1 and put into pot number 2 (the fast-color solution). The color will take immediately on the fabric which should be kept moving and in the dye for about 20 minutes. Shorter or longer time will depend on the color desired. (One artist does not stir the fabric at all.)

Finishing

Rinse through a number of cool water rinses to remove loose dye and dry. (*Note:* If deeper color is desired, fabric can be put back through the two baths. However, it must be rinsed before replacing in the Naphthol pot number 1 to remove any fast-color salts, which if carried into the first bath, will ruin the Naphthol solution.)

The two baths will keep for about 24 hours. Mrs. Bonner sometimes mixes more fast-color salt than she needs and finds that it keeps well in baby food jars in the freezer. When ordering Naphthol dyes, ask for a table to show the proportion of Naphthol and fast-color salts required for each color and for shades within the color. As with other dyes, amounts of fast-color salts used are proportionate to the weight of the fabric.

OTHER DYE SOURCES

Art teachers, constantly searching for materials that are "at hand and inexpensive" have discovered sources for aniline dyes other than those packaged specifically for fabrics. They are offered here because they may prove successful for others working under less than ideal situations.

Lucille Bealmer of Northern Illinois University offers the use of "ditto" paper for textiles and especially for batik. The purples and pinks of ditto paper dyes are difficult to obtain in batik dyes.

1. Tear a sheet of ditto paper into small pieces and place in measuring cup.
2. Add ¼ cup denatured alcohol. Stir.
3. Extend with hot water to about ¾ gallon and store as stock solution. Pieces of paper will float to top and can be removed.
4. Pour off color as needed and mix with cool water for dyebath.
5. Add salt and use.

Several artists report using aniline wood-stain colors sold in hardware stores under the name Rainbow.

Dissolve in alcohol or water, as above. Strain through cheesecloth. For dyeing, add salt. Experiment with amount needed for color desired, using proportions given on page 254.

Leather Dyes—Fiebings—Tandy's

Dyes used for applying coloring to leather are also aniline dyes with potential use for dyeing fabrics. They are available in liquid and can be painted directly on fabric; they can be diluted with water for dipping.

None of the above products have been tested for wash- and lightfastness. They should be experimented with on an individual basis.

DISCHARGE DYEING (*Bleaching*)

When you want to create a light pattern in a dark fabric or to lighten a dyed color, the discharge, or bleach out, process is used. Cotton, linen, and viscose rayon dyed with direct dyes and household dyes may be bleached. Fiber reactive dyes are resistant to bleach especially after they have been fixed. If you plan to bleach out color when using fiber reactives, do not use the washing soda or fixer until the final dyebath. Household bleaches can be used on many commercially dyed fabrics; always test strips before dyeing an entire piece. Never use bleach on silk, it eats up the fabric.

Fabrics to be bleached should be washed to remove sizing. They can be waxed for batik and tied for tie-dye. Vegetable oils such as Crisco, Mazola oil, and so forth, can be used for resists. Bleach does weaken the fibers so materials should not remain in the solution too long. Bleach fumes are very toxic; always work with ample ventilation. Bleach mixtures can be saved and reused.

HOUSEHOLD BLEACH: HOT SOLUTION FOR TIE-DYE

Use 10 parts water to 1 part bleach. Heat to just simmering and put the fabric in the hot solution and stir. Watch carefully until the fabric is the shade you want, then remove and immediately plunge into a cold vinegar bath of 3 parts vinegar to 1 part water. The vinegar will neutralize the bleach and help preserve the fabric.

COLD SOLUTION FOR BATIK AND/OR TIE-DYE

Strong solution—1 part bleach to 3 parts water
Normal solution—1 part bleach to 5 parts water

Always rinse and wash thoroughly after bleaching to remove all trace of the bleach that can destroy fibers. Also use prepared color removers such as: Putnam, Rit, Tintex.

Household bleaches will sometimes push the color and create dark edges which may be used advantageously in a design. Prepared color removers bleach out more evenly. If fibers are broken down from bleaching, a piece may be salvaged by cutting out the areas for negative shapes or using the good portions as appliqué.

Discharge methods can be used on paper. Experiment. Always keep an extra strip of paper with the same dye and bleach treatment and use for patching torn areas.

WILLY'S CAFE; SINCE 1865. Arnelle A. Dow. 22 inches high, 35 inches wide. Cotton duck. Whites, pinks, greens, and browns. Batik.

Courtesy, artist

DYE CLASS	BRAND OR DISTRIBUTOR	DYEBATH TEMPERATURE	ASSISTANTS	RINSING PROCEDURE	FINISHING
Fiber reactive (Procion) For Cotton Linen Silk Viscose rayon	Dylon Fabdec Fibrec Hi-Dye Putnam Color Fast	For batik and tie-dye at temperature 90°–100° Short and long dye procedures	Salt Washing soda (sal soda) for the reactive agent	After dipping or after fabric has dried	Wash in hot soapy water Ironing Steam treatment for direct application
Direct For Cotton Linen Viscose rayon	Aljo Dick Blick Calcomine Craftool (red label) Deka-Type L Fezan Keco-Direct Miyako 7-K	Hot dyeing at simmer 140° Adapted to cool dyeing 90°–100° Dye time 20 to 60 minutes	Salt	After dipping

After fabric dries After dipping After fabric dries After dipping | Wash in warm water

Ironing |
| *Acid* For Silk Wool | Aljo Craftool (black label) Fezan Keco-Acid (Keystone) Kriegrocene 7-K Miyako | Hot dyeing at simmer 140° or boil 212° Adapted to cool dyeing 90°–100° Dyeing time 20 to 60 minutes | Acetic acid (white vinegar)

Some also call for common salt or Glauber's salt | After dipping

After fabric dries After dipping | Steaming (optional)

Ironing |
Household (all purpose) For Cotton Linen Silk Wool Acetate Nylon Rayon and blends	Cushing's Perfection Dylon Multicolor Keystone Union Putnam all purpose Rit—liquid & powder Tintex	Hot but adapted to cool dyeing. Best for tie-dye at simmer Temp. 140°. Dyeing time 20 minutes. Can be used at cool temperature for batik but colors are not as bright as in hot dyeing	Salt Many have salt included so no added assistants necessary	After dipping	Iron while damp
Vat For Cotton Linen Silk Rayon	Inkodye	Room temperature for dipping and direct application. Dyeing time—a few seconds	None	Colors develop as fabric is exposed to heat and light	
Naphthol or azoic For Cotton Linen	American Hoechst GAF	For cool dyeing 85°. Dyeing time 20–40 minutes	Naphthol caustic soda Monopol Oil Fast-color salts Salt	After dipping	Wash in detergent and iron

HOW TO USE THIS CHART

Consult any given package of dye and determine the class. Then follow general instructions for that particular group regarding fabric, assistant, temperature, amount of dye and time. If a dye does not have the class specified, consult the known factors such as assistants required and directions for mixing, then determine the class and use the general instructions for dyeing.

APPENDIX

PREPARATION OF FABRICS FOR TIE-DYE BY MORDANTING

Fabrics should be washed in hot detergent water, rinsed and dried. Mercerized cottons need not be washed if new; mercerizing helps bind the dye and fabric.

Mordant is a French word meaning "to bite." Treating fabric with a mordant makes the fibers more receptive to the dye. It is not necessary, but some people feel it makes the color stronger and more light- and washfast.

Fabric can be mordanted only for tie-dye, not for batik. Fabric should be tied before mordanting and placed in a deep pot with enough solution to cover. Do not rinse out the mordant; it is most powerful immediately after it is removed from the mordanting bath and ideally should be dyed soon after it is removed from the mordant bath. If mordanted fabric is dried, the power is dissipated in a few days.

Mordant formula for 1 pound of fabric
For cotton, linen, and viscose rayon
    Place the fabric into the following solution:
        4 ounces alum
        ¼ ounce washing soda (sal soda)
        4 gallons soft water (add Calgon to water)
    Boil 1 hour and let stand in solution overnight.

For silk
   Place the fabric into the following solution:
      1 ounce alum
      1 ounce cream of tartar
      4 gallons soft warm water
   Stand in solution overnight (do not boil).

For wool
   Place into the following solution:
      4 ounces alum
      1 ounce cream of tartar
      4 gallons soft water
   Slowly bring to high simmer (never boil wool) and continue to simmer for 1 hour. Allow to cool in solution overnight.

CHEMICAL TREATMENT FOR WASH AND WEAR FABRICS BEFORE DYEING

(do not use on labels marked Perma-press)
   Mix ½ ounce hydrochloric acid
   2 gallons 190° water
Add fabric and simmer at 190° for 30 minutes. Rinse thoroughly.

HANDY CONVERSION TABLES

1 teaspoon	=		=	$\frac{1}{6}$ fluid ounce
3 teaspoons	=	1 tablespoon	=	$\frac{1}{2}$ fluid ounce
16 tablespoons	=	1 cup	=	8 fluid ounces
2 cups	=	1 pint	=	16 fluid ounces
2 pints	=	1 quart	=	32 fluid ounces
4 quarts	=	1 gallon	=	128 fluid ounces

Grams to ounces
   1 ounce = 28.35 grams
   1 pound = 453.60 grams

Cloth weight
   1 pound = 16 ounces

Melting points of waxes:

		flashpoint
Paraffin	90°	400°
Beeswax	120°	450°
Microcrystalline		
Mobil Wax® 2305	176°	540°

GLOSSARY

Acetic acid—A colorless liquid chemical compound used as the assistant for dyeing silks and woolens. Glacial acetic acid may be used. White vinegar is 5 percent acetic acid. Available: chemical and drugstores.

Acid dyes—A class of dyestuff for use on silk and wool. So called because they are used with acetic acid as the assistant.

All purpose dyes—See household dyes

Aniline—a colorless, oily liquid chemical used in making dyes, inks, varnishes, and other colorants.

Aniline dyes—Any dye made with the use of aniline; popularly any synthetic non-organic dye.

Assistant—A chemical mixed in the dyebath which assists the dye molecule to enter the fiber. Common salt is the assistant for cottons and linens. Acetic acid is the assistant for silk and woolen.

Baking soda—See sodium bicarbonate

Calgon—A trade name for a water-softening product. Available: grocery stores.

Caustic soda—Sodium hydroxide or lye used in mixing naphthol dyes.

Chemical water—Solution made for direct application of fiber reactive dyes combining urea, Calgon, and water.

Cold dyeing—Process of coloring fabrics in a bath of about 100°.

Cotton—A natural fiber obtained from the boll of the cotton plant.

Crackle—The characteristic veining created in batik by cracking the wax before dyeing.

Direct dyes—A class of dyestuff for use on cotton, linen, and viscose rayon.

Discharge dye—The process of bleaching out color.

Dyebath—The mixture of dye, assistant, and water into which the fabric is immersed.

Dyes—Soluble coloring substances that are absorbed by fibers.

Dyestuff—The dye particles before they are dissolved and placed in the dyebath.

Exhaust—To use up the color in the dyebath.

Fast-color salts—The dyestuff used in naphthol dye mixtures.

Fiber reactive—A class of dye designed specifically for cool water dyeing and mixed with salt and washing (sal soda) for use on cotton, linen, and silk.

Fixing—Setting the dye color.

Glacial Acetic Acid—A chemical compound used in photography which may be cut down with water by 30 percent for use as the assistant in dyeing silks and woolens. Available: photo suppliers.

Halltex—A trade name for an alginate thickener.

Hot dyeing—Process of coloring fabrics in a bath of 140° or higher.

Household dyes—A blend of several classes of dyestuff that can be applied to natural and man-made fibers and also to blended fibers.

Ikat—(Malaysian) A tie-dye technique where the yarn is tied and dyed before it is woven as distinct from tie-dyeing the whole fabric.

Linen—A natural fiber produced from the stem of the flax plant.

Lye—See caustic soda

Mercerized—A finishing process for cotton consisting essentially of impregnating the material with a cold, strong sodium hydroxide (caustic soda) solution which increases its affinity for dyes. Mercerized cottons should not be washed before dyeing.

Migrate—The moving or spreading of dye colors in areas where they were not applied.

Mordanting—Treating the fabric by soaking in a special solution before dyeing to make the fibers more receptive to the dye.

Naphthol dyes—A class of dyes also called Azoic and used on cottons and linens. Very fast colors supplied by fast-color salts mixed with caustic soda, Naphthol, and sulfonated castor oil.

Overdyeing—The process of dyeing one color over another.

Paste (to paste)—In dyeing, mixing the dyestuff with a little cold water before dissolving in hot water.

Pigment—An insoluble coloring matter that coats a fiber as opposed to dyes which are soluble colorants that are absorbed by the fiber. Pigments are usually opaque such as paints and enamels.

Procion—The trade name of fiber reactive dyes by Imperial Chemical Industries and ICI America, Inc.

Resist—The processes of blocking out areas of the fibers so they will not accept dye.

Sal soda (washing soda—soda ash—sodium carbonate)—Used as the fixing agent and reacting agent for fiber reactive dyes. Available: grocery stores.

Salt—Iodized—common salt that has been treated with iodine. In small quantities, it may be substituted for common salt.

Salt—Sodium chloride—in dyeing, used as the assistant for fiber reactive, direct, and household dyes. Common salt.

Silk—A natural continuous filament fiber obtained by unreeling the cocoon of the silkworm.

Sizing—Starch or other stiffeners present in new fabrics which must be washed out with hot soapy water before they can be dyed.

Soda ash—See washing soda and sal soda

Sodium alginate—A granular chemical compound used for thickening dyes. Available: chemists. Thickening mixtures available: textile printers and fiber reactive dye suppliers.

Sodium bicarbonate (baking soda)—Used for fixing in the cold printing application of fiber reactive dyes. Available: grocery stores, drugstores.

Sodium hydroxide—See caustic soda

Steaming—Moist heat process for fixing dye colors.

Synthetic dyes—Dyes derived from coal tar and other synthetic substances as opposed to dyes made from natural materials or minerals.

Synthropol—A trade name for a liquid detergent.

Thickener—A gel-like medium mixed with dyestuff and used in direct dye application and printing.

Union dyes—see household dyes

Urea—A solid crystalline compound used in the thickening formulas for dyestuffs. Available: chemical suppliers.

Vat dyes—For cotton, linen, silk, and viscose rayon. They are insoluble in water so must be dissolved chemically before applying to fibers. Colors develop under heat and light.

Vinegar—A sour liquid containing about 5 percent acetic acid which may be used as the assistant in dyeing silks and woolens. Available: grocery stores.

Viscose rayon—A manufactured fiber composed of filaments made of regenerated cellulose coagulated from a solution of cellulose xanthate. Viscose rayons can be dyed with some of the same dyes used for cotton and linen. The second class of rayon, called cuprammonium, will not take the same dyes.

Washing soda—See soda ash and sal soda

Wetting out—Thoroughly dampening the fabric before dyeing to assure more even dyeing.

Wool—Made from fibers obtained from the fleece of sheep or lamb, or from the hair of the Angora or Cashmere goat, the camel, vicuña, alpaca, or llama.

FOR YOUR INFORMATION

The following books, periodicals and other items are listed for additional information into the study and design of batik and tie-dyes.

BOOKS

Beech, W. F. *Fiber Reactive Dyes*. London, England: Logos Press Ltd., 1970.

California Design, Nine; Ten; Eleven. Pasadena, Calif.: Pasadena Art Museum, 1965, 1968, 1971.

Collier, Graham. *Form, Space and Vision*. Englewood Cliffs, New Jersey: Prentice-Hall, Inc., 1963.

Colour Index. 5 Vol. 2nd, 1956, 3rd Ed. Research Triangle Park, North Carolina 27709: American Association of Textile Chemists and Colorists, 1972.

D'Angelo, Anne T., and Windeknecht, Margaret B. *Batik Handbook—A Color Guide to Procion Dyes*. 1007 College Service, Houghton, Mich. 49931.

Graves, Maitland. *The Art of Color and Design*. New York: McGraw-Hill Book Co., Inc., 1951.

Hastie, Reid, and Schmidt, Christian. *Encounter With Art*. New York: McGraw-Hill Book Co., Inc., 1969.

Hickethiers, Alfred. *Color Mixing by Numbers*. New York: Van Nostrand Reinhold, 1970.

Hornung, Clarence P. *Hornung's Handbook of Designs and Devices*. New York: Dover Publications, 1946.

Johnson, Pauline. *Creating With Paper.* Seattle, Wash.: University of Washington Press, 1958.

Johnston, Meda Parker, and Kaufman, Glen. *Design on Fabrics.* New York: Van Nostrand Reinhold, 1967.

Maile, Anne. *Tie and Dye as a Present Day Craft.* London, England: Mills & Boon Ltd., 1963.

——. *Tie and Dye Made Easy.* London, England: Mills & Boon Ltd., 1971.

Meilach, Dona Z. *The Artist's Eye.* Chicago, Ill.: Henry Regnery, 1972.

Ogawa, Hiroshi. *Forms of Paper.* New York: Van Nostrand Reinhold, 1971.

Placek, Karl J. *Ornaments and Designs.* New York: Bonanza Books, 1971.

Robinson, Stuart. *A History of Dyed Textiles.* Cambridge, Mass.: The M.I.T. Press, 1969.

——. *A History of Printed Textiles.* Cambridge, Mass.: The M.I.T. Press, 1969.

BOOKLETS

A Dictionary of Textile Terms. Dan River Mills, 111 W. 40th St., New York, New York 10018 or Danville, Virginia 24541, 10th ed.

Batik Handbook: A Color Guide to Procion Dyes. By Anne A. D'Angelo and Margaret B. Windeknecht. 1007 College Ave., Houghton, Mich. 49931.

Fibers and Fabrics. By Josephine Blandford and Lois Gurel. U.S. Department of Commerce, Supt. of Documents, U.S. Govt. Printing Office, Washington, D.C. 20402.

Inkodye. Screen Process Supplies Mfg. Co., 1199 E. 12th St., Oakland, Calif. 94606.

Naphthols on Cotton Yarns. GAF Corporation, Melrose Park, Ill. 60160.

Procion Dyes-Printing. De Montfort Press, Leicester and London, Great Britain.

PERIODICALS

CIBA Reviews
#58 Batiks
84 Maori Textile Techniques
95 Cotton
96 Velvet
104 Plangi-Tie and Dye Work
113 The Wool Fiber
1967/4 Japanese Resist Dyeing Techniques
1969/1 Alginates
Ciba Ltd., Basle, Switzerland. These are no longer published but can be found in many libraries.

Craft Horizons: American Crafts Council, 44 W. 53rd Street, New York, New York 10019.

Handweaver & Craftsman: 220 Fifth Ave., New York, New York 10001.

Shuttle, Spindle and Dyepot: Handweavers Guild of America, 339 N. Steele Road, West Hartford, Conn. 06117.

Textile Chemist and Colorist: Journal of the American Association of Textile Chemists and Colorists, P. O. Box 12212, Research Triangle Park, N.C. 27709.

Textile History: Published annually by David and Charles, South Devon House Railway Station, Newton Abbot Devon, England.

ARTICLES

Craft Horizons: August 1971, Vol. 31, #4.
      Article: Lois Brooks. Workshop: Adire Eleko, pp. 12–14.

SLIDE KITS

Slide Kits available from American Crafts Council, 29 W. 53rd St., New York, New York 10019. Send stamped self-addressed envelope for rental information.
Tie-Dye, 1972. Historical and contemporary examples. 67 slides.
Javanese Batiks, 1970. The collection of Jane Gehring. Mainly historical. 60 slides.
Tie-Dye Techniques, 1972. Eileen Richardson demonstrates various approaches to tie-dye. 80 slides.

SUPPLY SOURCES

Many local art and craft stores carry batik supplies. For specific dyes and distributors around the country, the following are listed for your convenience. No endorsement or responsibility is suggested by the author. For additional suppliers consult your local telephone classified pages under art, craft, and hobby shops and under dyes. Industrial dye distributors buy dyes in large barrel drums and normally charge for repackaging in small quantities.

Aiko's Art Materials 714 N. Wabash Avenue Chicago, Ill. 60611	Miyako direct and acid dyes, tjantings, wax, rice and starch paste components, Aritex, dye crayons
Aljo Manufacturing Company, Inc. 116 Prince Street New York, N.Y. 10012	Direct dyes, acid dyes, thickening powders, tjantings, wax
American Art Clay Co. Rub 'N Buff Division Box 68163 Indianapolis, Ind. 46268	Colored batik wax
American Hoechst Corp. Main Office 129 Quidnick St. Coventry, R.I. 02816	Naphthol dyes
Bareco Division 6910 W. 14th Street Tulsa, Okla. 74115	Microcrystalline wax
Binney & Smith, Inc. 380 Madison Avenue New York, N.Y. 10017	Crayola crayons available in local stores

Glen Black
1414 Grant Avenue
San Francisco, Calif. 94133

Fiber reactive dyes, thickeners, wax, tjantings, urea

Dick Blick Art Materials
P. O. Box 1267
Galesburg, Ill. 61401

Dick Blick dyes, Putnam dyes, wax, tjantings, batik frames, alcohol lamps, pigments

Stephen Blumrich
Rte. 1—Box 25A
Halsey, Or. 97348

Calcomine direct dyes, tjantings

Bona Venture Supply Co.
17 Village Square Shopping Center
Hazelwood, Mo. 63042

Versatex Textile Paint, Dorland's Paste Wax, pigments

Art Brown & Bros., Inc.
2 W. 46 St.
New York, N.Y. 10036

Dyes. General batik supplies.

CCM—Arts & Crafts, Inc.
9520 Baltimore Avenue
College Park, Md. 20740

Direct dyes, wax, tjantings, alcohol lamps, batik frames, Someil dye crayons, pigments

Craft Kaleidoscope
6412 Ferguson Street
Indianapolis, Ind. 46220

Dyes. General batik supplies.

Craftool
1 Industrial Road
Woodbridge, N.J. 07075

Direct dyes, acid dyes, tjantings, wax, batik frames, alcohol lamp

W. Cushing & Co.
North Street
Kennebunkport, Maine 04046

Cushing's Perfection Dyes; all purpose; wax, tjantings

Dadant & Sons, Inc.
Hamilton, Ill. 62341

Beeswax—large quantities

Dharma Trading Co.
1952 University Ave.
Berkeley, Calif. 94701

Fiber reactive dyes, thickeners, waxes, tjantings, frames, unsized cotton

Durable Arts
Box 2413
San Rafael, Calif. 94901

Versatex textile paint, Dorland's Paste Wax, pigments

Dylon International Ltd.
139–151 Sydenham Road
London, S.E. 26, England

Dylon Multi-purpose
Dylon Fiber reactive

Earth Guild/Grateful Union
15 Tudor Street
Cambridge, Mass. 02139

All dyes, tjantings, waxes, thickeners, brushes. Unusual catalog: $2.00

Farquhar Fabric Dyes
6 Clarence Square
Toronto 135, Ont., Canada

Empire–White Products Co.
45 Herman Street
Newark, N.J. 07105

Rainbow aniline dyes

Fabdec
P.O. Box 3062
Lubbock, Tex. 79410

Fiber reactive dyes

Fezandie & Sperrle, Inc.
103 Lafayette Street
New York, N.Y. 10013

Fezan direct dyes, Fezan acid dyes

Fibrec
2815 18th Street
San Francisco, Calif. 94110

Fiber reactive dyes, thickeners, waxes, tjantings, 1¾-ounce package. Will package in larger quantities on request.

GAF Corporation
1950 N. Hawthorne Avenue
Melrose Park, Ill. 60160

Naphthol dyes

Keystone Aniline & Chemical Co.
321 N. Loomis Street
Chicago, Ill. 60607

Dyes: fiber reactive, direct, acid, union. Minimum 1-pound packages. Packing charges.

Keystone–Ingham Corp.
13844 Struikman Road
Cerritos, Calif. 90701

Dyes: fiber reactive, direct, acid, union. Minimum 1-pound packages. Packing charges.

J. C. Larson Co., Inc.
7330 N. Clark Street
Chicago, Ill. 60626

Dyes: direct, acid, Putnam, fiber reactive Dylon. Wax, tjantings, frames, alcohol lamps, batik frames, Versatex Textile paints, Dorland's Paste Wax, pigments.

Le Jeune, Inc.
1060 W. Evelyn Avenue
Sunnyvale, Calif. 94086

Hi Dye—fiber reactive, thickener, wax

Magnus Craft
109 Lafayette Street
New York, N.Y. 10013

Wax, tjanting, alcohol lamps, batik frames

Mobile Oil Company
612 S. Flower
Los Angeles, Calif. 90065

Mobil wax 2305 microcrystalline wax —also available from sculpture suppliers

Bryan Mumford
P.O. Box 14649
U.C.S.B.
Santa Barbara, Calif. 93017

Tjantings

Northwest Handcraft House Ltd.
110 W. Esplanada
North Vancouver, B.C., Canada

Fiber reactive, direct acid dyes, fabrics: raw silk, unbleached cotton

Polyproducts Corporation
13810 Nelson Avenue
Detroit, Mich. 48227

Magic™ Batik

Putnam Dyes
Quincy, Ill. 62301

Putnam all purpose dye in soluble packets. Putnam fiber-reactive also available in local drug and grocery stores.

Pylam Products Co.
95–10 218th Street
Queens Village, N.Y. 11429

Fiber reactive dyes

Resin Coatings Corporation
14840 N.W. 25th Court
Opa Locka, Florida 33054

Remyzist

RIT
Best Foods Division CPC International
1137 W. Morris St.
Indianapolis, Ind. 46206

Rit all purpose powder and liquid dyes. Available in local grocery and drugstores.

Rupert, Gibbon & Spider
470 Maylin Street
Pasadena, Calif. 91105

Deka type L direct dyes

Alexander Sanders & Co.
Route 301
Cold Spring, N.Y. 10516

Microcrystalline wax

Sax Arts & Crafts
207 N. Milwaukee
Milwaukee, Wis. 53202

General supplies and dyes

Screen Process Supplies
1199 E. 12th Street
Oakland, Calif. 94606

Inkodye, wax, tjantings, Indian Head cotton

7 K Color Corp.
927 N. Citrus
Hollywood, Calif. 90038

Dyes: direct, acid, special fluorescent dyes

Stein Hall & Co.
285 Madison Ave.
New York, N. Y. 10017

Halltex (sodium alginate)

Test Fabrics Inc.
P.O. Box 53
200 Blackford Avenue
Middlesex, N.J. 08846

Unsized fabrics

Toadstool Studios
1739 W. 99th Street
Chicago, Ill. 60643

Large pine stretcher frames illustrated on page 48

Lee Ward
840 N. State
Elgin, Ill. 60120

Colored wax, wax, unsized cotton

Zimmelri, Sandra and Martin
26 Tower Street
Jamaica Plain, Mass. 02130

Naphthol dyes, tjantings, wax, cotton

INDEX